# *Fender*
## STRATOCASTER

# Fender
## STRATOCASTER

SAM ORR

THE CROWOOD PRESS

First published in 2009 by
The Crowood Press Ltd
Ramsbury, Marlborough
Wiltshire SN8 2HR

**www.crowood.com**

British Library Cataloguing-in-Publication Data
A catalogue record for this book is available from the British Library.

ISBN 978 1 84797 101 2

This book is dedicated to Louis Jack Chapman, Jamie Thaddeus Folta and Charlotte Amber Wishlade
(the next generation of guitar players); also current players for the inspiration, Wesley Emanuel
Leon, Timothy James Chapman, Jerome Lee Scott, David Lewis and Stewart Alexander Orr.

Typeset by Sara Millington Editorial and Design Services
Printed and bound in Singapore by Craft Print International

# ACKNOWLEDGEMENTS

Suzy Watson, Stewart Orr, Paul Watson, Eileen Orr, Sally Orr, John Orr, Kay Orr, Wes Leon, Tim and Maria Chapman, Lewd and Iona Lewis, my 'homeboy' Jerome Lee Scott, John Lewis, Gillian Lewis, Mother Lewis, Cath and Brian Chapman, Guy, Liz, George and Alice Bengree, Edward Burnham, J.C. and the Townsends, Aunt Pat (RIP), Ted Tibbles, Kitty Tibbles (RIP), Steve Aird, Paul Aird, Tom and Allie Barnett (here's one for the bath Tom...), Phil Baxter, Adam Bearcroft, Ben @ Beej Guitar Repairs, Francis Body, Ellie Seller, Brady Jones, Brandon and the Silk Pigs, Samantha and Emma Brown, Rufus and Emily, John and Liz Seller, Surya Buck, Joe Buck, Charlie and Marianne Buck, John, Jools and Hargi from Carpet, Jamie and Owen Clegg, Martin Ellis at City Bar, Jo Condon, Steve Cosgrave, Nigel Crinson, Hannah Dale, Rachael Dent (read it all now...), Nathan Hale Langley, Tony at the Frog, Chris Edwards, Tim Foxon, George, Kate and Jamie Folta, Mark Gibson, Trevor Greenhalgh, Rob Hambling and Family, Ryan Heath and Family, ACCK, Liz Beardshall, Jim and Hedda Morrow, James Hill, Simon Hunter, Paul, Ella and Charlotte Wishlade, Tom Huxley, Erin Hyde, Clare Walker and Innocent Gun, Jamie Jones, Matty Jones, Mike Kay, Graham Kay and Family, Keiron Lewis, Dan Kelly, Sean Kelly and Family, Leah Simone, Fei Leung and Family, Richard/Dennis Linley, David Joseph George Smallman, Gary Lloyd, Tommy Lloyd, Bernie Marsden, Maxwell and the Owens, Simon Hughes, Nick Murphy and the Ferriswheel Junkies, Alex and Charles O'Brian, Brian McCabe, Neal and Mother of Six, Paulio, P.J. from Dawsons, Owain John, Tony Resteux, Carl Ridge, Alex Irvine, Simon and Sarah Rodriguez, Mark Rogers, Tim Ryan, Andy and Emily Singleton, Andrea Steele, Steve and Lisa Toye, Daniel Steinhardt, Timmy Taco, Leon 'The Forg' Joinson, Tom and Chris Drury, Matthew Thomas, Christian and Mel and Hellmouth, Brett 'Musty' Malkin, John and all the Weatherleys, Andy Wishlade and Family, Caesar Glebeek, Jim Marshall, Leo Fender, Jimi Hendrix, A.R. Duchusoir, Les Paul, Orville Gibson, Donna Leech, Alex Dooley, Lisa Fortune, Mike Devoy, Ms Lydon (the best English teacher), Dan Kellaway, Adam and Justin at Music Ground, Chris and Alison Edwards.

There are many more acknowledgements I may have missed out, please find me and complain!

# INTRODUCTION

Fullerton, California, October 1954. Leo Fender and Co. is busy fulfilling purchase order #242 for 100 units. These units are to become the archetypal electric guitar icon. It is doubtful whether it crosses Leo's mind that what he has just put into production is to be the most successful electric guitar ever made. The aura surrounding the first 100 units is to make these among the most desired guitars in the world today, all hand-crafted by a small group of Californians more than fifty years ago.

The Fender Stratocaster has influenced, inspired and given the world some of the greatest music ever played, from 1950s rock 'n' roll through to 1970s punk and 1990s funk.

The beauty of the Fender Stratocaster to anyone who has ever laid fingers on either a maple or rosewood fretboard is that the guitar itself creates the player. The tone, sound and feel of each individual instrument is completely different to the next. For that reason alone it's fair to say that the Fender Stratocaster has a distinct right to be exactly where it belongs. The Stratocaster is burned into the memories of the older generation as more than just a piece of nostalgia, held up to the dreams of the current generation as a piece of history to own.

1954 was the year of the Stratocaster, an icon born from economy. The guitar featured a highly attractive two-tone sunburst finish, mainly to expose the ash wood grain body, which was selected for its appearance as well as tonal and lasting qualities. The neck was made from one piece of solid maple and the interchangeable electronics had a drop-in assembly. Above all, and by accident, it had great looks. The guitar was loaded into a brown leatherette-covered wooden case with a plush rouge lining and shipped out to music stores across the USA, priced at $249.50

A 1960s Stratocaster for sale at $37,000. RRP on this would have been around $300.

The vintage guitar market has grown with the Stratocaster's popularity.

**Modern guitar shops usually stock around ten types of Stratocaster.**

The guitar retailed for around ten per cent more than Gibson's Les Paul Gold top model and around thirty per cent less than a top of the line Gibson Les Paul Custom. Fender had hit the nail on the head when it came to knowing the market. One of the main draws and selling points of a Fender Stratocaster was, and has always been, the synchronized Tremolo, a feat of engineering able to emulate tremolo sounds at no extra power and bend notes to any desired pitch. This feature still makes guitar luthiers scratch their heads in amazement. Never have the two words 'simple' and 'effective' met so graciously.

Throughout the 1950s the Fender Stratocaster changed very little, apart from the guitar's body being changed to alder wood in mid-1956. Cosmetically the guitar was exactly the same, although from the technical view it became more and more playable due to the pointers given to Fender by endorsees and cus-

tomers. There was a distinctly happy accident when one of Fender's employees took a few days off and left the neck-sanding job to a less experienced member of the workforce. The next thing to happen was a big meeting to discuss a batch of necks that had been sanded completely wrongly! Should they scrap the lot or let them go out and hope for the best? They decided on the latter and no complaints were heard. This accounts for some of the easily recognized guitars of 1957. During 1958 the Fender Stratocaster received a notable cosmetic boost, when the original two-tone sunburst finish became three-tone. The colour was a great hit, except that the red hue in the new finish was easily scared away by sunlight and all the 'new' guitars become very old, very quickly.

Another cosmetic or running repair job throughout the Stratocaster's history has been the choice of plastics used in manufacturing. The original plates, pickup

The Telecaster has followed in popularity and price.

covers, knobs and tips were made from a very brittle and impractical plastic. This is very evident on Buddy Holly's famous Stratocaster made in 1955; it looks as if a good part of the cover has been sanded away to reveal the black bobbins underneath. This type of fake Bakelite was replaced with a more durable plastic soon after. In typical 'waste not, want not' Fender fashion, some guitars from this period have both old and new types of plastic. This distinguishing feature makes them highly sought after.

The 1960s brought the Fender Stratocaster to the UK and into the hands of a newly arrived Jimi Hendrix. It is known that Fender sales were not at their best in 1966 when Jimi Hendrix came along. He has been described as the Stratocaster's saviour, since at the time it was falling out of favour to Gibson's Les Paul model.

The considerable changes made to the Stratocaster during the 1960s are also featured in this book. Half-

way through this decade the CBS Corporation took control.

It would be fair to say that this decade saved the Fender Stratocaster and its music seared its way into the mind of every guitar player. From then on the guitar's status continued to grow to its present glory – modified, repainted, exported, smashed, burned and always cherished.

The Stratocaster stood proud next to Levi's jeans, Cadillac cars and Wurlitzer jukeboxes. And it is amazing that in its modern state the Stratocaster can still be regarded alongside iPods, LCD televisions and upmarket Aston Martin or Mercedes-Benz cars. There are not many things designed and built in 1954 that remain incredibly popular and still sell in almost unimaginable numbers. The Stratocaster has carved out its own empire, manufactured in Japan, China, Mexico and Indonesia as well as in the USA.

The first landmark point in my life focused around a particular Stratocaster came around Christmas 1992, when my father presented me with a half-size, left-handed 'Stratocaster' copy. I turned it upside down, mainly due to my fascination with the way Hendrix played, but it didn't last too long in my hands as I grew pretty quickly and did not want to be seen with what, to all my friends, was a 'toy' guitar. My next Stratocaster-style guitar was a Squier Stratocaster in black with a maple neck, purchased following years of begging my parents. It cost £85 second-hand from a music shop I would later work at. It became my baby – I'd eat with it, take it to school, watch TV with it and even sleep with it when my mother told me she'd take it away if I didn't go to bed!

I became obsessed with Strats, drawing them, writing about them, tinkering with the electrics after learning how to use a soldering iron at school. I'd ask for money from all angles for birthdays and Christmas every year until I could buy more Stratocasters. I then moved on to Mexican models and in 1997 eventually traded all four of my guitars for the one, an American Standard Stratocaster. The moment the shop told me I could have a USA Stratocaster I nearly jumped for joy, then remembered to act calm so as not to ruin a deal that ended with me owning a 'genuine' American Fender Stratocaster. All the work I had put in, modifying, saving and begging, had paid off. I rushed home with a moulded black Fender case in my hand and ran upstairs, opened the case and sat on my bed speechless. It was sonic blue, maple neck, serial number N7207847. I drew the guitar in my art book at school with the name 'Skye' underneath it; this was my pride and joy. I loved the guitar and still remember the smell of the case when I first opened it. I urge anyone with this guitar to contact me as I'd love to have it back. Many a Stratocaster fan has let a good Strat go and this was my downfall. I used Skye for two years, but I then discovered Stevie Ray Vaughan and decided that under no circumstances could I go without Fender's SRV model. This became the next chase. I worked my way towards getting the cash together, even owning a 1979 hard tail model in the meantime. I part exchanged all of my gear in Farnham for a second-hand one that I rebuilt back to its original specification, but quickly fell out of love with it – all at the age of fourteen. I have owned well over 100 Stratocasters in my life but it's the early ones that had all the magic. I now own only one Stratocaster, which you will read about later.

There is a lot more I could say on glorifying the Stratocaster or my own Stratocasters, but I will leave you with this: this is no toy. You can make a living off it, you can swap, sell or buy it readily, you can mess around with it, you can do what you like with it – but rest assured, for the rest of everyone's lives the Fender Stratocaster will be in recording studios and stadiums around the world, glossed up on magazine covers, dulled down in newspapers, and close to the hearts of guitar players around the globe. Here is the link between Jimi Hendrix and Nils Lofgren, Robert Cray and Howling Wolf, Eric Clapton and John Mayer, Yngwie Malmsteen and Peter Green, and, last but not least, you and me.

# 1950s ERA STRATOCASTERS

The 1950s era Stratocaster is an absolute work of art and Strat lovers the world over consider the first 1954 Stratocasters to be the 'holy grail'. The guitar evokes nostalgia, rock 'n' roll, Cadillacs, bubble gum and a pivotal time in the twentieth century. The majority of 1950s Stratocasters were finished in a thin coat of nitrocellulose in a two-tone sunburst colouring. This means the edges of the guitar were black, blending nicely into a brown and yellow combination. The body is always beautifully finished and there is a solid, one-piece maple neck. All this beauty was contained within a brown leatherette and red plush interior hard shell case, and cost a grand total of $249.50 with tremolo or $229.50 without. These guitars were made up of the following pieces.

## Body

This part of the guitar was built using two pieces of either ash or alder, which was introduced in late 1956. The types of wood were carefully chosen: ash, for example, has notably attractive grain properties that also make it easier to book match the two body parts, giving a stunning effect in either a blonde or sunburst finish. The bodies on early Stratocasters, including the 1954, were hand-sanded, with the result that each and every one would vary in thickness of depth from body to body. Other points that vary are rear contours, which may be deeper or shallower. Deeper contours are favoured in these models as there is less overall weight to the complete guitar. The original idea for a contour body came from a local player named Bill Carson. He had used an early Telecaster in his swing bands and found that the body dug into his ribs too

much, making it uncomfortable to play. When designing the body of the Stratocaster, Leo took this into consideration and began taking more and more wood off the back of the new guitar until it was comfortable enough for Bill. This then became a prominent feature in the Stratocaster's design.

Underneath the pick guard on these Stratocasters you will find routing for the electrics, while closer to the bottom on the body you should see a 'wiring well', which is a simple yet effective route for all the pickup wires to travel down and not flex the pick guard. There are also two extra holes drilled for earth wires to the rear and jack socket. (Note that hard tail Stratocasters are earthed at the bridge, not the rear tremolo claw.)

Due to the high water content and density of ash, the Stratocaster body weighs substantially more in ash than in alder, but players could decide on whether to pay extra for a custom colour and a little more weight. The guitar's finish was the standard two-tone sunburst, but for an extra five per cent to the retail price you could have a custom paint job on your brand-new Stratocaster. One of the first custom colours to be ordered was Fiesta Red. With different automotive colours being very popular at the time, Fender decided to try and match the guitar to these colours, thus cementing a lasting bond between the two icons of popular culture. George Fullerton has said:

> One day, I went down to the local paint store and I started to explain to the man what I had in mind. I had him mix some paint there on the spot and finally we came up with a red colour and that particular colour became Fiesta Red. In England, that was the only colour they bought for a long time, they weren't ordering anything else, but that Fiesta Red.

Here is a clean late 1950s Stratocaster; this model shows a blonde refinish and a fair bit of wear on the maple fingerboard throughout.

The rear of the blonde late 50s Stratocaster – the refinished examples usually show very little wear to the body, but unless the neck has been refinished too, the guitar can look a little odd.

This finish in Fender's catalogue appealed to all at a time when other guitar companies around the world were staying with either natural or sunburst finishes. Fender had found a niche market for wildly coloured guitars. Rumour has it that Fender made a custom colour for the Las Vegas bandleader Hank Penny: solid purple! Another early customer for a custom colour Stratocaster in the 1950s was Eldon Shamblin, a player on the western swing circuit, who requested a gold finish. When delivered the Shamblin Stratocaster turned out to be a fine instrument, although on recent inspection it has now oxidized and turned an interesting shade of green. A custom colour Stratocaster from this era would today be a highly prized and expensive instrument. Costs can easily escalate over £50,000 for an example in a condition suitable for museums.

The bodies on these guitars have the same pin routes on the beginning of the top body horn and adjacent on the bottom of the body. The pin routes, which were used to keep the body stable while being cut out of a larger piece of alder or ash, are great telltale signs of counterfeit Stratocasters. The holes are about the size of a pinhead, hence the name, and were then filled and hidden discreetly in the black of a two-tone finish. Towards the end of the 1950s, Fender attempted to add another blend of colour to its sun-

This mid-50s Stratocaster is in remarkable condition and shows a rich two-tone sunburst finish with little wear all over.

burst finish, a translucent red to fit neatly between the yellow and black of a standard model. Bill Carson, who worked for Fender at the time, remembered having to search out various types of paint following the introduction of the third tone, when complaints began coming in that the red paint pretty much vanished after a little contact with UV sunlight rays! The story goes that, in an attempt to stop this happening, Fender began testing pieces of alder with the paint and leaving them on the factory roof to see if any of the red would fade; one type managed to keep its colour and so it was used for the rest of the production. You could have 1950s Stratocaster bodies either with or without tremolo fitted. Both models are equally great guitars: with the non-tremolo model you get slightly more sustain and neatly drilled and ferruled holes for string ends, simply brilliantly designed: on the other option you get a fantastic tremolo effect at your fingertips with a great resonant, if primitive, spring reverb unit built into the back. An average 1950s model Stratocaster is in itself a thing of timeless beauty and modern art. Much of this is due to the wonderful hand-shaped body and beautifully finished paint when in mint condition. Even when completely torn up after years of gigs and life on the road they hold a place in the heart of any Strat player.

## Neck

Made of maple, with a walnut strip running from the body end of the neck up to about the second fret, the neck was built and then shaped by hand. The necks on very early 1954 guitars are quite large in the hand and come complete with twenty-one small frets. Some early 1950s models have highly figured maple (known as 'flame' or 'bird's eye'), but this is purely coincidental. Leo Fender was not keen on using highly sought-after figured wood owing to its rarity; it would be more practical and cost-effective to use standard maple on the production mill on early Fender Stratocasters. The headstock of each guitar does tend to vary with depth but not as much as the bodies. The logo is another point to make most Strat players go weak at the knees. It comprises an elaborate 'Fender' logo outlined in black with a gold interior and a straight block font 'Stratocaster' following. Underneath these two logos you should find the words 'With synchronized Tremolo' in a font similar, but smaller, to the Stratocaster logo. The 'Fender' part was a more coherent version of Leo Fender's signature. On the rounded tip of the headstock it reads 'Original Contour Body' in a style hand-drawn by the wife of one of Leo's closest friends. The tuners are placed six in a line on one side of the headstock and a truss rod adjustment can be made at the body end of the neck. Adjustment means removing the neck on a Stratocaster. The other end of the headstock has a walnut plug. These necks were signed in pencil on the body end, followed by a date of manufacture. These are commonly seen with 'T.G.', which stands for Taddeo Gomez, an employee who is now a cult celebrity in vintage Stratocaster circles!

As with the bodies, the necks were finished in a clear nitrocellulose lacquer that has since aged to a beautiful golden colour. During the early years of production, players found problems with the fingerboards of their Stratocasters when, after a few years of playing, the lacquer on heavily used frets would wear through and look unsightly. Other features to the neck of an early Stratocaster are the plain black plastic dots on the fretboard as position markers; these are featured as single dots up until the twelfth fret, when

The neck of the mid-50s Stratocaster shows the usual signs of aging, mainly from the 'G', 'B' and 'E' strings.

two are present. Also present on the headstock of an early Stratocaster is a single rounded string tree. This was to ensure correct tension and keep either the 'B' or top 'E' string from popping out of the nut during heavy playing. Rounded string trees caused a little friction to tuning and were changed to a 'butterfly' style, which has a tiny washer underneath. This was not really noted by players and was more than likely a small manufacturing cost saving.

Throughout the 1950s the necks were changed considerably, in shape and feel more than aesthetically. A happy accident happened in 1957 when an employee accidentally sanded a V-shaped neck and continued to produce a whole batch with the new shape. Upon inspection, Fender could not decide what to do, whether to pull them all back or let them go out and see if anyone complained. Needless to say, they all went out and none were returned. This neck shape is in use to this day and is still highly sought after in early models.

Towards the end of the 1950s, while aesthetically changing the Stratocaster's finish with the extra colour tone in the sunburst, Fender decided to address the problem of worn fingerboards. They rectified the problem by using a thin veneer of rosewood on the maple neck. This was accompanied by clay dots instead of the black plastic that had been used on plain maple. This not only worked, helping to solve the problem of aged fingerboards, but gave the Stratocaster a completely new look.

Whereas early maple necks had the truss rod inserted through the back of the neck and filled in with the

walnut stripe and headstock plug, the new rosewood one would make life less complicated with the truss rod being installed at the front of the neck and covered over with the new rosewood fingerboard. These guitars seem to be a pivotal point in the Stratocaster's history and design.

## Plastics

The early Fender Stratocasters used a smaller design than commonly seen and all the knobs, pickup covers and switch tips were a lot more rounded in shape. Fender then moved production material over to bakelite for knobs, pickups covers and switch tips, but due to its tendency to become brittle it was abandoned around 1955 for a more durable plastic. An early example of the Bakelite guitars can be seen in Buddy Holly's Stratocaster, with its worn pickup edges and rounded knobs. The plastics all tended to become yellow with age or turn a slight cream colour as opposed

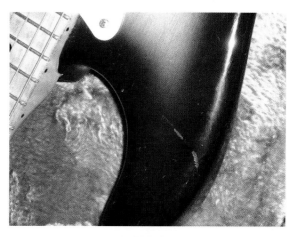

The plastics on this early Stratocaster show that Fender's move away from Bakelite plastics to avoid premature aging was a worthy one.

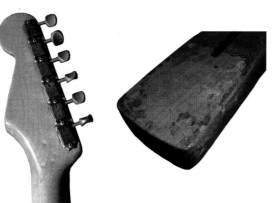

These pictures depict the rest of the mid-50s Stratocasters age points – the body has minor wear on the edges and the rear of the neck shows little wear. The headstock rear is in remarkable condition for its age and the neck heel shows lacquer loss; this usually occurs when a neck is removed from the body for the first time due to pressure from the four bolts.

to the brilliant white they once were. The back plate covering the tremolo springs on these guitars originally had the serial number stamped onto it, but this was then moved to the chrome neck plate. The switch tip from this era has gained the nickname of 'football', as it resembles an American football.

On the early models the pick guard, which was held to the body by only eight screws, tended to warp over the years. This was standard throughout the Stratocaster's early life until players and Fender began to notice the warping. The next stage began in late 1959 when Fender began making a three-ply pick guard with eleven screws holding it in place.

Early Stratocasters are easily identified by the wear on the plastics.

## Pickups and Electrics

Every pickup, being the main soul of a Stratocaster, is specific in its own way; each example from the 1950s has as much individuality as the guitar it is attached to. From the beginning the pickups were hand wound. Those employed to do this supposedly wrapped the individual windings around each bobbin, but this is not the case. While Stratocasters of the 1950s are renowned for their 'hand-wound tone', the image of Fender employees winding each and every individual wire that this phrase inspires was not as it sounds. The pickups themselves were held in place in a machine that spun the wire on to the pickup. While every pickup received close to its correct number of turns, using this method it was necessary for the wire to be guided onto the pickup by hand. Pickups that got more turns usually sound slightly hotter or punchier than the standard type. Each pickup on the 1950s era Stratocasters required around 8,350 turns.

**OPPOSITE AND OVERLEAF: Here is a refinished blonde 1954 Stratocaster; this particular example is 100 per cent original except for the finish, which suits the overall appearance of the guitar. The neck heel is pencil-dated by the mythological Taddeo Gomez, who has made some of the best 1950s necks and has never been seen since Fender's early days. This type of Stratocaster is a worthy inclusion to any guitar collection. Note the round string-retainer.**

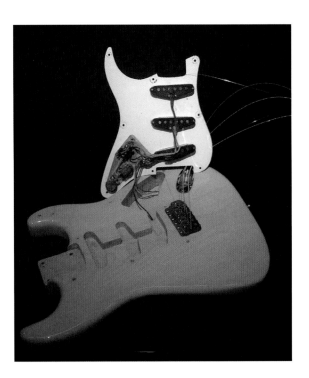

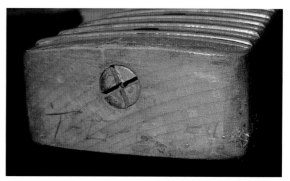

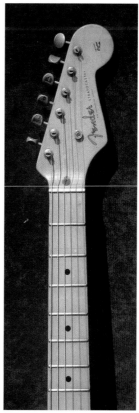

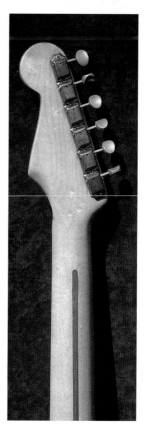

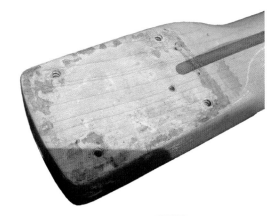

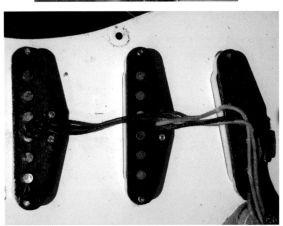

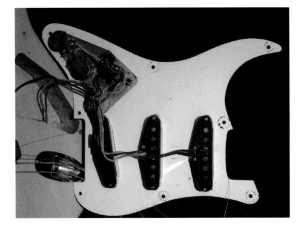

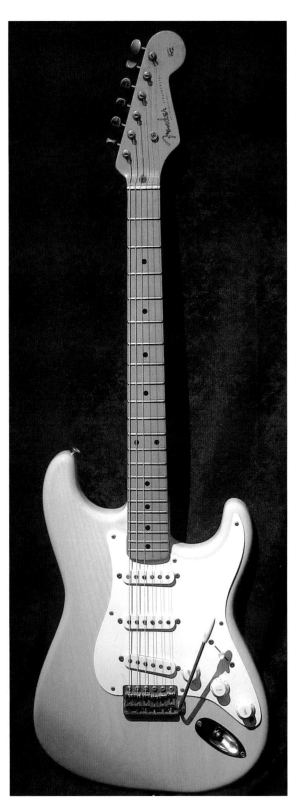

Alnico magnets are named after their composition, which contains aluminium, nickel and cobalt as well as iron. This gives the overall tone of a 1950s Stratocaster a quite metallic sound that has become associated with the era.

The pickups have a unique way of aging. Over the years the pickups slowly lose a fair bit of their punchy sound and acquire a great sounding, full tone. These have ended up being highly sought after.

The 42GA Formvar wire used on the 1950s era Stratocaster has thicker insulation than usual, resulting in a slightly larger pickup body. This is useful when identifying an original instrument.

The original configuration of the Stratocaster's electric components consisted of three single coil pickups, a three-way selector switch for activation of each pickup, one master volume for all three pickups and two tone controls for either the neck pickup or the middle pickup.

The pickups themselves were powered by six individual alnico V magnets, which were staggered in height to add overall volume of each string whether it is a thick E string or a high B. The order of the magnets, from shortest to tallest, is as follows: B and E magnets (treble); G and E (bass); and A and D. Before 1956 the largest magnet on each pickup was the D magnet and this is another good telling point for an original example.

The electric components on early Stratocasters are shielded from interference radiated from neon signs, fluorescent lights and other electrical items. The shielding consists of a small triangular metal plate to keep interference to a minimum. This is one feature that Fender has continued to improve to the present day by various means.

The potentiometers on early Stratocasters are graded 250K ohms each. The controls for both volume and tone are known as potentiometers, the difference being that the tone pots are wired together whereas the volume is mainly used as an earth and is connected to the switch and pickups. Stratocaster potentiometers of the 1950s have codes labelled on them. (To see how the codes correlate to the date of manufacture, please see the reference section below.) Middle tone potentiometers on the 1950s era Strato-

caster have one 1. MFD capacitor at their heart; these are commonly orange coloured and are cylindrical with a value code printed on it in black ink.

Switches used during the 1950s are branded CRL and were usually constructed using brown-red fibreboard.

The wire used to connect all of the electrics in these guitars was cloth covered and was either black or white, depending on its use: earth wires are always black, whereas the live wires are white. This wire is very easy to work with as its shielding is easy to strip back without using wire strippers.

## Hardware

Early 1950s Stratocasters have the first effective individual saddle adjustment seen on any guitar. The saddle on each of these guitars has PAT. PEND stamped on it, since the patent on the design had not been granted at the time of the saddle's manufacture and also to warn off anyone thinking of creating a similar saddle and putting it on their own brand of guitars.

The bridge unit of the Stratocaster comprises nine parts: the block (painted light grey), the base plate, six individual saddles with two small grub screws on each either side of the string path, and six screws and springs with screws to attach to the base plate. This mechanism with the block was topped off with a separate tremolo arm, three or five springs, spring claw and two adjustment screws. The block and base plate are attached with three short Philips-head screws. The bridge gained a touch of flair in 1955 with the addition of a snap-on chrome-plated cover intended to cover up the apparently 'unsightly' bridge, which could sometimes become worn and sharp, making it quite uncomfortable for the player.

Machineheads or tuners manufactured by a company called Kluson were used by Fender and Gibson throughout the 1950s. The early 1950s Stratocaster tuners did not feature a Kluson brand name on the rear cover, but this changed in 1957 when the words 'Kluson Deluxe' were stamped on the cover with the 'O' acting as a maintenance hole for oil to keep the tuner lubricated.

Here is an early 1950s Stratocaster in two-tone sunburst finish. The wide grain on the body is typical of ash wood, which was used for its weight and grain. Ash adds a dynamic sound to a Stratocaster and, especially with a maple neck, the sound can be very bright. You can see how tarnished the bridge and saddles are on these photographs – a well-used but cared-for guitar. Note the worn rear of the body, and the cracked Bakelite pickup covers and knobs.

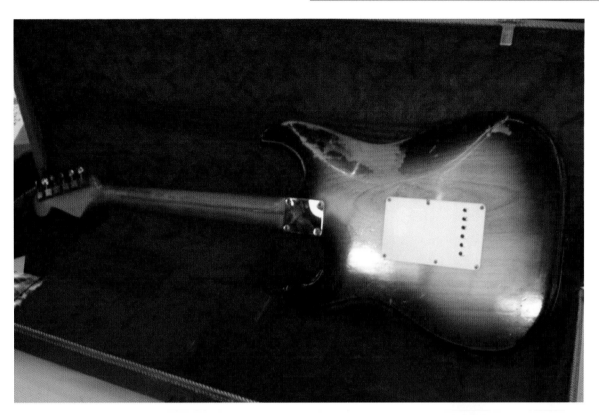

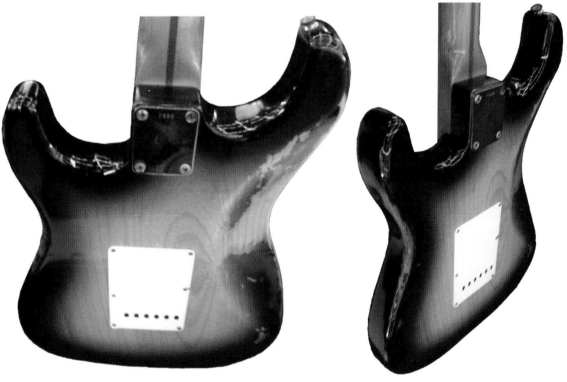

**LEFT AND OPPOSITE:**
Here is a clean late 50s,
left-handed Stratocaster
in its original tweed case.
Three-tone sunburst
examples in this condition
are becoming highly
sought-after.

Unfortunately the Philips screws from the 1950s Stratocasters, with different sizes for the pick guard and neck plate, do not have any codes or specific markings to help identify them when placed alongside their modern counterparts.

## Case

The guitars were supplied, as an optional extra, in form-fitting wooden cases covered in brown leatherette with red plush interior. The cases themselves are almost as revered as the guitars they housed.

About 1955 the Stratocaster's case was changed for a more luxurious tweed model. One theory suggested for the change is that Fender had been making tweed-covered amplifiers for some time and wanted to incorporate this into the Stratocaster's aesthetics. Since the form-fit cases would not take the tweed eas-

ily, owing to its shape, Fender decided to make cases that were rectangular, thus giving the player a larger accessory compartment than the earlier form-fit example. This also enabled Fender to incorporate the tweed into the Stratocaster. The new rectangular case had brown leatherette ends to keep the tweed from fraying and the same red plush lining. The hardware for the cases was the same as for the form-fit model except that the handles, which were formerly made from Bakelite, were now manufactured from wood covered in leatherette.

The company that made these cases for Fender is known as C+G cases. It is only recently that they have started advertising this fact with a small badge on the accessory compartment lid near the leather fastening.

The 1950s era Stratocaster is a highly prized instrument in is own right, and given the sum of its parts it is still one of the coolest guitars on the planet. The names associated with the 1950s Stratocaster are

synonymous with guitars and rock and roll music the world over. Such figures as Jeff Beck, Eric Clapton, Steve Marriott, Buddy Holly, Jimmie Vaughan and David Gilmour have helped increase the value and notoriety of 1950s Stratocaster guitars. As they become rarer and more valuable by the year, it is increasingly evident, to Stratocaster guitar fans or general musos alike, that a 1950s era Stratocaster, whether in pristine condition or road worn, is a sight for sore eyes. If one is ever placed in your hands, it will repay close inspection of its parts and deep reflection on its history.

This late 50s Stratocaster has a beautiful two-tone finish, which remains intact to show how well-crafted the early Stratocaster bodies were. The guitar has a sweeping contour and perfectly formed body horns.

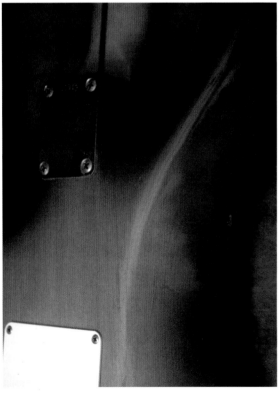

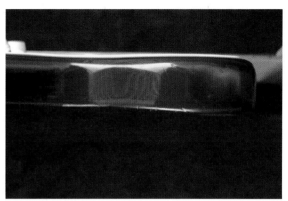

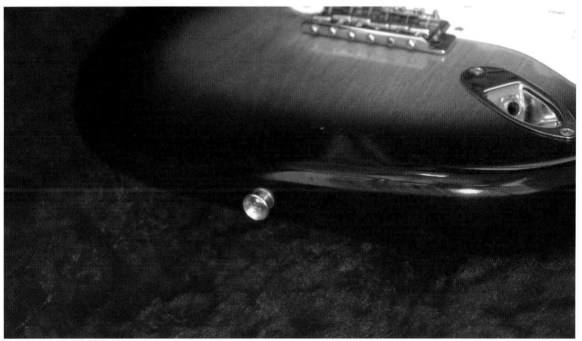

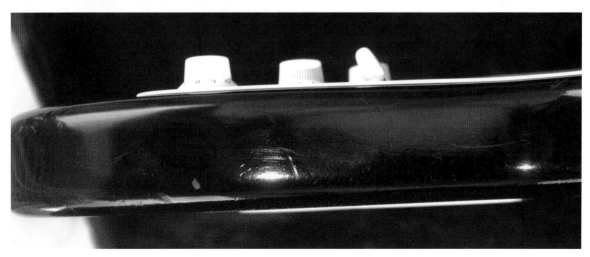

A clean 1950s Stratocaster, this is exactly the type of guitar that fetches sums over £20,000 from dealers and auction houses worldwide.

This '57 Stratocaster shows Bakelite plastics that have aged considerably. Many reissues of this type of Stratocaster come complete with cream plastics to mirror the age of original models such as this.

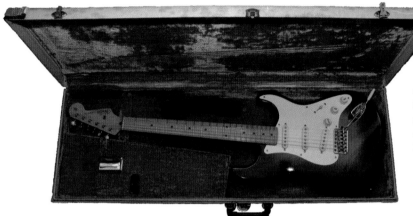

A road-worn, late 50s Stratocaster in three-tone sunburst in its original tweed case, complete with ashtray bridge cover.

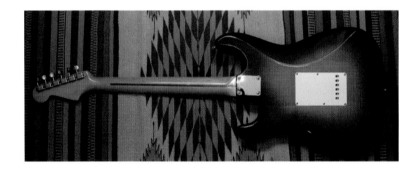

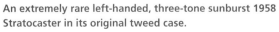

An extremely rare left-handed, three-tone sunburst 1958 Stratocaster in its original tweed case.

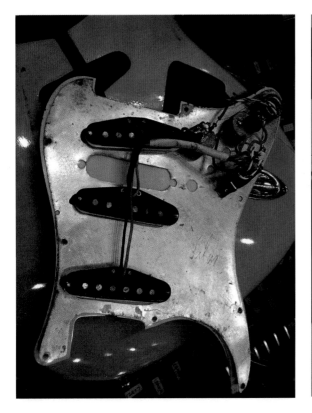

An unfortunate Stratocaster that has been through various modifications. This type of Stratocaster does not fetch the prices of cleaner examples. The electrics have been considerably altered and the guitar has been through more than one refinish. Oddly enough, the metal shielding plate indicates that the owner has installed a fourth pickup in the past. This type of modification can demand a new pickguard if the owner wants to return the guitar to its original state.

An original tweed case with accessories. These are normally missing from an early Stratocaster but can add considerable sums of money onto the final price of a guitar.

# MODERN ALTERNATIVES TO VINTAGE COUNTERPARTS

Buying a vintage Fender Stratocaster is out of most people's reach due to their cost and scarcity. The vintage Fender Stratocaster has become a severely hot item on account of how few original models from the 1950s and 1960s (and surprisingly even from the dreaded 1970s) survive. Many people have tried to recreate the sounds they hear on 1950s and 1960s records in painstaking detail. Tribute bands for such acts as The Shadows, Buddy Holly and Jimi Hendrix come under serious criticism from guitar buffs and aficionados if they attempt to get away with using such instruments as a Squier Affinity Stratocaster or a similar inferior copy, tone-wise and in appearance.

Guitars from these periods have become such a commodity that criminal gangs roam the world, pinpointing certain valuable models and making organized efforts to steal them. With prices ever escalating, such guitars have become so closely guarded by their owners that they rarely see the light of day and are touched only once a year. It would be interesting to ask Leo Fender whether he had any idea that the working man's guitar of choice would become the connoisseur's pride and joy. I bet that the answer would be an abrupt 'No'.

This all adds to the magic of Fender's Golden Child. Owning a vintage model is a rare thing. Indeed buying one is restricted to those with £15,000 burning a big hole in the pocket.

Fender is not a company to let this type of problem slide.

During the late 1970s Fender received reports that the original models from the 1950s and 1960s were fetching very good money and that players preferred the various neck sizes, body shapes and finishes. This did not faze the company at all. Besides, they were busy developing their own Strats with garish finishes and various hardware options. The problems arose when a Japanese company called Tokai bought a bunch of vintage Fender Stratocasters and began recreating them down to the last detail (*see* Chapter 8).

## American Vintage

When these guitars finally came to Fender's attention, they set about developing their own models that would encapsulate the feel and tone of a vintage Stratocaster. The two models that Fender settled upon were the 1957 Fender Stratocaster and the 1962 Fender Stratocaster. These were chosen purely for the aesthetics of the years themselves: unless you show an undying love for Chevrolet cars, for instance, a '57 Chevy sounds a lot 'cooler' than a '53 Chevy. So Fender used 1962 for the same reasons: a '57 Stratocaster is by no means better than a '58 Stratocaster.

The Vintage Reissue Stratocasters, as they are known, or American Vintage series have been a steady seller for Fender since they were introduced in 1983. Guitars from this period, however, were not perfectly accurate, the body shapes were a touch bulky and neck shapes were a bit odd, but since they were made in the original Fullerton factory, they too are now collectable and rare.

The Vintage Reissue Stratocasters today are pretty good replicas of the models: they hold their own live, they contain all the magic of owning a real Fender Stratocaster and they sound and play beautifully. Some even have cheeky bits of flame maple on the necks; these are somewhat rare but pleasant to see!

## Japanese Vintage

Around the late 1980s the Vintage Reissues made in the Fullerton factory still had fierce competition from the Japanese market guitars, especially Tokai. For a time it looked as if Fender's action in creating a USA model of an original Stratocaster had proved successful, but then figures came in on how many Tokai 'Stratocasters' had been sold, especially for export. Realizing that Tokai had a monopoly on the sub-£500 vintage-style Stratocaster, Fender fought back by commissioning a Japanese factory and replicating Tokai's impressive output. The Japanese Fenders were born and were given the brand name Squier. These guitars are, in a word, great. They seemingly followed the original Stratocaster down to the last detail. They had the look, the neck, the colours, the tone and, above all, they were cheap. These Japanese Squiers are affectionately known as the 'JV' series, which stands for Japanese Vintage. Having the name 'Fender' anywhere on this guitar (below the name Squier) made the JVs an instant smash hit with players looking for a cheap Strat that played like a dream and sounded superb, while the JV was a wonderful replacement for vintage collectors too frightened to take their beloved '63 Strat out for a gig.

After the success of the JV Stratocaster, Fender Japan began following the USA factory by making and exporting reissues. It is still a mystery why Fender allowed this. The early reissues were classed as the 'Collectables' series. They included 1950s and 1960s Stratocasters, a 1968 Stratocaster and a 1970s era Stratocaster. The guitars were also available in all the right classic colours: Surf Green, Daphne Blue, sunburst, black, white and, weirdly enough, Salmon Pink! Fender again got it right and the guitars are still coveted by players and collectors alike. These guitars have instant appeal to any Stratocaster lover. For a start they look right, and to many players that is important. Now your Hendrix tribute band can have a white '68 Japanese reissue Stratocaster and not worry about it being stolen, as it only cost £400 and not the £12,000 you would have to save for an original.

## Mexican Classic

In early 1998, after a good ten years of exporting the wonderful Japanese reissues, Fender took the operation away from Japan and opened a brand new facility just across the border in Ensenada, Baja Mexico. The plan was to make cheaper reissue models in the Mexican factory and take over the market dominated by the Japanese models. These were to be known as the 'Classic' series. They are still available in most good guitar shops and are priced roughly around the £450 mark. They include a 1950s model available in two-tone sunburst, black, white, Fiesta Red (originally a limited edition, but it has remained in the catalogue since 2005), Surf Green and Sonic Blue. The 1960s model is available in three-tone sunburst, black, Lake Placid Blue and Burgundy Mist. During the first years of production the 1960s Classic was available in Olympic White, but this has been discontinued. There is also a 1970s Classic Stratocaster available in white, black or natural. These have either maple or rosewood necks. These models make for great Stratocasters with a gig bag included in the price. There really is no reason not to inspect one when in the market for a good, affordable Stratocaster.

Savings are made by cutting costs on various components, including the wiring, woods and electrical components. The question commonly asked about all these models and factories is 'What's the difference?' The simple explanation, as any fool will tell you, is that you won't get a better guitar than the sum of its parts although they are all trying to do the same job – be a good Fender Stratocaster. Japanese reissues, for example, are great guitars with good overall structures, good neck pockets and great looks, but are let down by their inferior electrics. The Mexican Classics are also let down by inferior electrics, but they do have good bodies, necks and pickups. If you aim to spend between £350 and £500 on a Fender Stratocaster you'll get exactly that for your money. If you up the budget to £1,000 or £1,500 you will get a Stratocaster of much higher calibre. The American Vintage Reissues come in a rainbow of colours that to this day are sprayed on in nitrocellulose paint, which is a lot thinner than the thick polyurethane paint used on the Japanese and Mexican models. This allows a lot more resonance and over time it will begin to look like an original battle-scarred Stratocaster from the 1950s, 1960s or (since 2007) 1970s. A cheaper model will not look as authentic since it has not been made and finished as an original.

Instead of a padded gig bag, with the £500 model you now get an authentic plush-lined brown or black Tolex case (with the 1960s or 1970s models) or a crisp tweed case. You also get cloth wire inside the electronics. Great workmanship can be seen on all three types of reissue, but the USA model has the edge. It also possesses the Fender magic as a brand new Stratocaster from the original country and company that invented the world's most popular electric guitar. This sounds a lot more appealing than either a brand new Stratocaster from Japan or one from Mexico. Good Strats have been made in the USA since day one. This is why Eric Clapton has never used anything else. The same goes for Hendrix, Mayer, Beck, Gibbons, Gilmour ... the list is endless. The others are good replicas but the USA Stratocasters are great guitars.

## Fender Custom Shop

Going further up the bank loan, at the top of the pile of alternatives to a vintage Stratocaster are the Fender Custom Shop models. These guitars win hands down in any competition. They arrived on the scene about 1995 and have been a huge success, since Fender will quite happily scratch the finish, burn the headstock, corrode the hardware and basically make it look well used. These guitars are seriously good. Unfortunately Custom Shop guitars also seem to come with serious price tags. The Custom Shop will sell you whatever Stratocaster your heart and big wallet desires. At present they do 1956, 1960 and 1969 Strats. (A 1965 Stratocaster with the ever-cool 'transition' logo headstock has been discontinued.) These guitars feature select alder bodies, flame, bird's-eye or plain maple, African rosewood, Indian rosewood, proper electronics, switches, wiring and hardware and, above all, workmanship. The overall guitar is exceptional and you know that, given the quality of its build, it will outlive most other guitars. But, alas, the price puts off an awful lot of people. The usual starting price of around £2,000 is enough to make people run a mile, but all Stratocaster fans are aware of them and their overall ten out of ten marks for effort against an original 1960s or 1950s Stratocaster.

Each guitar is made by a team of skilled luthiers in California and is issued with a signed certificate stating its serial number and the Custom Shop president's signature on the bottom. The guitars are next in line to the exclusive club of great Stratocasters and sound the business in the right hands. You can have the models in an array of finishes: NOS (New Old Stock) has the appearance of a guitar made that week; Closet Classic is aged so that the guitar looks as if it was bought in its respective year and has been played lightly until the present day; while Relic gives every impression of having been used all its working life, with scratches, cigarette burns and aging hardware.

The Fender Custom Shop is truly a Mecca for guitarists with the resources to buy a replica Stratocaster. If you have the money and patience, the Custom Shop will create any type of Stratocaster you want. Perhaps you fancy a blonde 1964 Stratocaster, slightly tatty but still looking great, that you saw in a guitar magazine years ago. They'll do it. A black 1983 American standard? Done.

The Custom Shop has also teamed up with the Mexican factory to produce interesting guitars known as the Classic Player Stratocasters, available in 1950s or 1960s styling. It is interesting to note that these guitars have been designed by the Custom Shop master builders Dennis Galuszka and John Cruz. They are good alternatives and are definitely worth a look for those shopping for the best Stratocaster from Mexico.

## Taking it Further

The other problem with having a good alternative to a vintage Stratocaster is that, if you spend a few hundred pounds on a Japanese or Mexican Stratocaster, there is always the temptation to make it better: new pickups, pots, wire, switches and pickguard. After all, that's why they are built that way – to alter, customize and modify. The Japanese and Mexican Strats are excellent candidates for upgrading parts, but players rarely realize the full extent of their cost: a decent set of pickups could cost you up to £300; decent electronics might be over £100; and finding someone capable of performing all the good work on your brand new Stratocaster could set you back another £100. By now you have spent nearly £1,000 on a Mexican Stratocaster, when you could have bought a USA Reissue for another £100. The links go on and on until you reach either the Custom Shop or you're standing in a vintage guitar shop with £15,000 in your hand! Who said buying an electric guitar was easy?

I have heard many a tale in guitar shops of people claiming to have the world's best Stratocaster: 'I've got a Squier Strat, paid £100 for it and it's the best Strat in the world, bar none. I've tried Custom Shop, USA Vintage etc ...' From what people say, it appears that having the 'best Strat' is largely a matter of personal preference and not having the money to buy the one you really wanted more than anything. I play a Custom Shop Stratocaster. I have owned nearly a hundred Stratocasters in my life. A few have come close, but none has ever been quite as good as this. Yet I would happily hand it over for an original model from 1968 or 1969 if the chance came up, and if it played well and sounded good. I have played Strats that cost £500 less. I have played Strats that cost £1,000 less. But my trusty old black '69 NOS Stratocaster is my personal favourite. It has some history, scars, burns and stickers, but to me it's still number one. It is because I'm proud of what I have achieved as a player and feel I can justify the price tag to my bank account. That's all. Your Stratocaster may be your favourite and may have cost you a third of the price, but at the end of the day everyone has their favourite and personal taste is unique.

The next time you hear someone claiming to have the best Stratocaster, just think how many Stratocasters out there are probably better than theirs – even in their eyes. It is what makes playing, buying and owning Stratocasters such a unique experience. Guitar shop bravado is hot air at the end of the day. It is also best avoided.

We all await the next Stratocaster that floats our boat. When it arrives, we'll be there in the shop, staring, playing and dreaming about it. It's what has made the Stratocaster so successful over the past fifty years and will continue to well into the next fifty years and beyond.

# PICK AND MIX STRATOCASTERS

This chapter looks at Stratocasters that are not well known and appear to have slipped through the net. Some of the guitars featured are ultimately very rare indeed and are never seen outside collectors' vaults. They are held in high regard by players and collectors and I have included prices for each in case you should ever feel the need to purchase one.

## Stratocaster Plus

The Stratocaster Plus was in production between 1987 and 1996. The guitar is a typical 1980s or 1990s model and was the first of the deluxe Stratocasters. It was the first production guitar to feature Lace Sensor pickups as standard. The guitar won the *Music and Sound* award for innovation in 1989.

### BODY
The body was manufactured from solid alder and was identical to that of an American Standard of the period apart from the unusual finishes, which included Graffiti Yellow.

### NECK
The neck was available in either maple or rosewood. Unlike that of an American Standard model, it has an LSR roller nut, a friction-reducing device used on early guitars to improve tuning stability. The LSR nut was later replaced by a unit designed by Trevor Wilkinson, a British-born manufacturer of advanced hardware for guitars, who currently designs units for Vintage guitars in the UK. The new nut featured needle-bearing rollers at string contact points.

### HARDWARE
The inclusion of Sperzel locking machine heads, together with the roller nut, made the Stratocaster Plus the most stable non-locking tremolo guitar Fender had ever made. The guitar also featured the famous two-point tremolo, which had been a big success on the American Standard Stratocaster.

### ELECTRICS
The three Lace Sensor pickups on the Stratocaster Plus were the first to be fitted to a Fender guitars. Don Lace, who passed away in 1992, created a single coil-sized pickup that, instead of single pole pieces, contains multi-magnet pickup alternatives. These were intended to give a good single-coil tone without the dreaded hum that has plagued the Stratocaster for many years.

Don Lace also manufactured a Dually Lace pickup, which worked on the same principle as the previous Lace pickup but was humbucker-sized.

The Stratocaster's new pickups have a semi-artificial tone that many Stratocaster purists feel does not make a good-sounding guitar. After playing one, however, they may concede that Fender got it right for the market. The Stratocaster Pplus also incorporated the TBX tone circuit, which added a lot more signal thanks to the Lace Sensor pickups.

Should you be in the market for a Stratocaster Plus, the price as of 2008 is usually in the region of £600.

## Rosewood Stratocaster

In 1968 Fender built a few guitars completely out of rosewood as limited runs. These included George

Harrison's infamous Rosewood Telecaster, which can be seen in the Beatles' rooftop performance at the end of *Let It Be*. Years later the Telecaster was reissued by the Custom Shop as a limited run in 2007. The Telecaster was followed, also in 1968, by two completely rosewood Stratocasters. One was built by Philip Kubicki and intended as a gift for Jimi Hendrix, but it never made it to its master's hands and it is not known what happened to it. The other rosewood model was made as a prototype to eventually go into production, but the realization that it weighed in at 11lb (5kg) probably put Fender off; it would have outweighed a Les Paul – another Fender first!

In case your dream of acquiring one of these guitars, either the one Hendrix missed out on or the prototype, should ever become reality, be prepared to dig deep because ... the sky is the limit.

## Paisley and Blue Flower

## Stratocasters

The humble Paisley Stratocaster first popped up in late 1969 just as flower power and paisley were becoming essential items for the home or fashion. Fender followed with a Telecaster and Stratocaster decorated with either blue flower pattern or paisley. The paisley design was a firm favourite of James Burton at the time he played backing guitar for Elvis in the early 1970s. The paisley and blue flower patterns were achieved by pasting wallpaper to the guitar's body and then profusely lacquering it to give a painted effect. The effect was also applied to the pickguards of these guitars.

The paisley and blue flower guitars were available from Fender USA between 1969 and 1979. They were later mass produced in Japan; these versions normally feature a 1950s-style neck and headstock, although a few have emerged with the correct construction for the 1970s. Japanese manufacture has now been discontinued and relatively inexpensive examples can normally be found.

Estimated prices (2008) for the different models are in the region of:

| | |
|---|---|
| 1969 Paisley Stratocaster | £8,000 and up |
| 1970s Paisley Stratocaster | £5,000 and up |
| Japanese Reissue Stratocaster | £300 |

## Lucite Stratocaster

Very little is known about the Lucite Stratocaster. The rarest and possibly the most expensive of all Stratocasters, it was designed in 1957 and took four years to complete. It is constructed out of Lucite, a transparent plastic, and was meant for promotional use at trade shows. The guitar itself is completely see-through, showing every aspect of the Stratocaster's insides: truss rod, electrics, bridge and tremolo unit. *Guitar Player* magazine has described it as 'the most valuable non-celebrity solidbody Fender ever made'. With its Lucite construction, the guitar is most definitely not for the working musician since it weighs 18lb (8.2kg). As of 2008 it is in a private collection ... so don't even think about a price, because it won't happen!

## Zebra-Wood Stratocaster

The Zebra-wood Stratocaster is a favourite of mine, as well as of numerous guitar players worldwide. The guitar was originally made in 1969 and only a few exist. It features a completely double-bound and chambered body that incorporates stained zebra-wood into its grain. The guitar also has a bound neck with block inlays, which add a Gibson touch to an outrageous Stratocaster. There is a strong visible grain on the body.

The guitar has the usual Stratocaster layout but has a different edge to it that does not appeal to everyone. Originals are never seen for sale, but if one were to come up for auction, expect to have to bid around £20,000.

### REISSUES

The Zebra-wood Stratocaster is held in high regard by Japanese enthusiasts. A Japanese version with very good build quality is now in production and it is possible to pick one up for close to £900.

# THE BRITISH INVASION

Britain had emerged victorious from the Second World War, but the enormous cost of damage and loss set the country heading towards economic turmoil. The United States of America offered a $4,336 million line of credit and a lend-lease loan of $586 million to cover costs, but this had to be repaid over fifty annual instalments beginning in 1950. Payments were deferred on six occasions because of economic or political crisis; the last payment of $83 million (£45.5 million) was finally made to the USA in December 2006.

When the first commercial Stratocasters came on the market in 1954 they were normally only available to USA customers and to very wealthy customers worldwide. The UK mostly had to make do with cheap European imports such as Hofner and Framus, although Stratocasters arrived in very small numbers brought by travellers and seagoers. The UK later had Burns and Vox guitars, which came to be seen as the norm. No one could get their hands on a nice shiny Fender until 1959.

A few American guitars could be found at this time, however, and it is reported that Lonnie Donegan found a Gibson Kalamazoo in Selmer's music shop in Charing Cross Road, London, and later a tatty Martin acoustic for the bargain price of £6. He took his Gibson on National Service with him in 1949.

When Rock 'n' Roll music really kicked off in the 1950s, music retailers experienced a severe increase in demand for guitars. This was exactly the time for the European floodgates to open, and anyone who was anyone had a cheap Hofner or Framus. A favourite was the Hofner Club 50, which was favoured by, amongst others, the session guitarist Joe Brown, later a rock legend in his own right. Joe had been using a Hofner until a slick cherry red Gibson ES-335 made its way into his hands! This was in 1961, again at Selmer's

in Charing Cross Road. As you can well imagine, he was more than happy with his red 335, and he used it heavily on all his session work from then on. Unfortunately Joe later sold the 335 and it now belongs to Roy Wood.

The first Stratocaster to hit the UK with a bang was bought by Cliff Richard for his lead guitar player in the Shadows, Hank Marvin. After gazing at Buddy Holly on the cover of an LP, Hank decided that the guitar he held was the one to have, so when Cliff asked Hank about his dream guitar the answer was easy. Adhering to Hank's demands, a fresh Fender catalogue was ordered and Hank and his friends went about ordering the best Stratocaster possible. First of all it had to be red – not just any red but Fiesta Red (a custom colour). It had to have bird's-eye maple (a costly extra) and it needed gold hardware (expense isn't the word!) The guitar eventually arrived and Cliff and the band stood around staring in amazement at this instrument, which could only be described as 'a piece'. This guitar was and still is considered the Holy Grail by Shadows and Stratocaster fans all over the world. It is now owned by Bruce Welch, to whom Cliff presented it in thanks after helping to revive his career in the 1970s.

The guitar reached Cliff's hands when restrictions on the importation of luxury goods from the USA, introduced in an effort to improve the country's balance of payments, were lifted around 1961. Jennings/Vox Industries became the sole importers of Fender products. The Shadows were sold on a set of Fenders in matching Fiesta Red finishes. Being the early 1960s, these were all rosewood models. The idea was possibly stolen from Gene Vincent, who had his Blue Caps using blonde 'Mary Kaye' Stratocasters and a matching precision bass.

So begins the legend of Selmer and Jennings. Jennings were the first to get hold of Stratocasters and they couldn't get enough. The usual sunbursts turned up with a few in Fiesta Red. With guitarists by nature being very peer-led, from the word go everyone wanted a red one like Hank's. So your average sunburst model was left behind. Having a red Stratocaster was the epitome of cool.

Jennings decided to refinish a few sunburst models in a similar colour to Fiesta Red using a semi polyurethane mix. It is worth noting that Jennings turned the neck plate round so the serial number was upside down on the rear. These guitars are actually quite rare. The other odd feature is that Jennings would not supply the Fender case with your new Stratocaster. Instead it was an expensive extra, although for less you did have the option of a Jennings case. This was a bad fit but its beige Tolex-style covering, in the same material that was then used on Vox amplifiers, could be considered a cool feature. The interior for these cases was a dark ruby red plush with a small accessory compartment. Despite this, having an original blonde or brown Tolex case was a serious must for every player, but only achieved at great expense.

Later in the decade Selmer, which had a long history of manufacturing and supplying musical instruments, began to sell Stratocasters and supply their own case, which was also used by other guitars at the time. The cases supplied by Selmer were in a timeless snakeskin outer covering with a rich, blue plush lining.

Once a Stratocaster had been found, the other problem was getting replacement strings. The main strings available were Black Diamond strings, hated by most players and used only grudgingly. These were followed by Cathedral, which were a vast improvement.

Being around Charing Cross Road at this time must have been a great experience. The small number of great guitars that passed through the area were quickly adopted by such greats as Peter Green with his '59 Gibson Les Paul, Hank with his Stratocaster, Eric Clapton with his Les Paul and Cherry 335, and Jeff Beck finding another '59 Les Paul for a few hundred pounds.

Interestingly enough, Rory Gallagher managed to get his hands on a tasty sunburst Stratocaster in Ireland thanks to a show band guitar player who insisted the Stratocaster he ordered had to be red like Hank's and traded in his brand new sunburst one for the privilege.

Unfortunately musical instruments had been included among the luxury goods subject to import restrictions. In the case of Fender's products, it appears this had the effect of building a pent-up demand, especially when such stars as Buddy Holly were seen on the emerging television channels playing what seemed, at the time, unique, modern or futuristic instruments. When the ban was lifted it is thought that the UK took most of Fender's Stratocaster model for several years and, as a result, early 1960s models are more common in the UK than the USA. The vast majority of early 1960s Stratocasters are also in Fiesta Red finish.

The archetypal British Stratocaster fits the following description: Fiesta Red refinished body with a slim early 1960s neck, a Jennings or Selmer case, paired with a clean Vox AC30 amplifier, and strapped on a player in a mohair suit.

And so it was that the Stratocaster had finally invaded Britain.

**OPPOSITE AND OVERLEAF: Here is a typical British Stratocaster. The vibrant Fiesta Red finish is offset beautifully against the Mint Green of the pickguard. This type of Stratocaster is very common in the UK due to the Shadows and Hank Marvin's influence on the nation's guitar players. You can see in the photos how the body is very rounded in certain areas, making this specific guitar unique. This particular example is pencil-dated 1961 and is 100 per cent original, right down to the Jennings of London case, which is covered in VOX AC30 material, a cheaper alternative to the Fender case which was separated from its guitar when imported.**

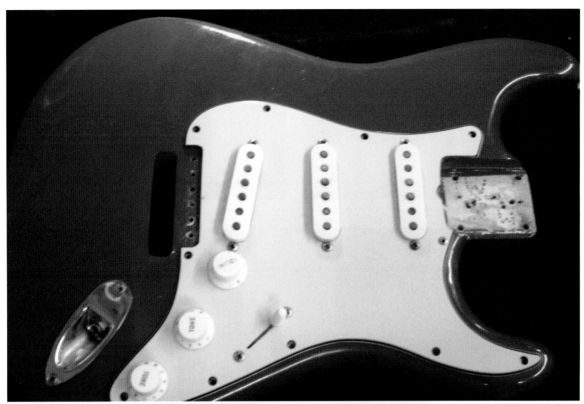

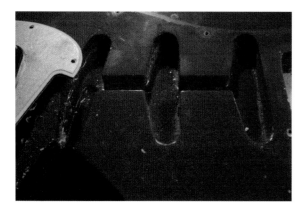
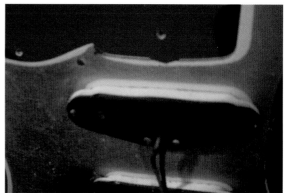

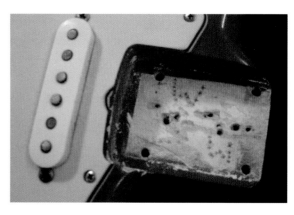

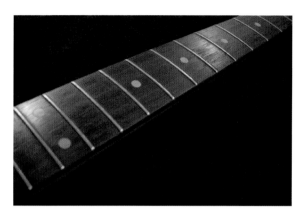

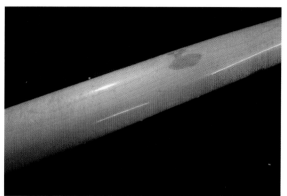

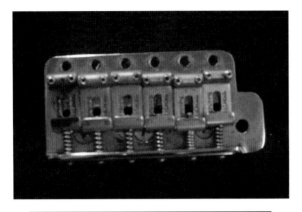
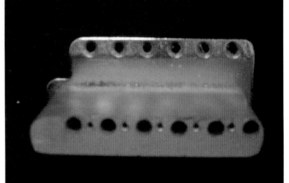
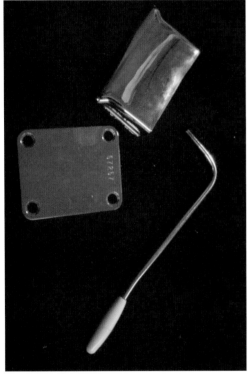

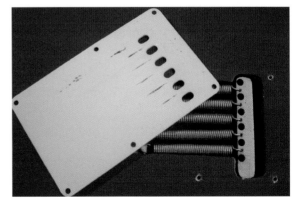

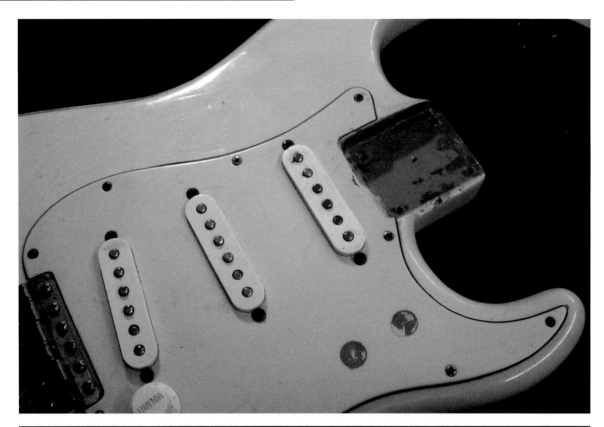

Here is a 1961 Stratocaster that was originally Fiesta Red when it first arrived in the UK. This specific guitar has undergone many modifications in its time, including a complete neck and body refinish, newer pickups, new volume pot, and at one time mini switches were added but have since been removed and the holes filled. This guitar is one of the best Stratocasters I have ever laid hands on.

# 1960s ERA STRATOCASTERS

The 1960s era Fender Stratocaster is a different animal to its 1950s counterpart, with an abundance of distinctive changes both cosmetically and internally. At the NAMM show in July 1958 Fender had introduced the Jazz master guitar, which was a much flashier model than the Stratocaster and featured Fender's ill-received floating vibrato. This was both a blessing and a curse for Fender, since it made the Stratocaster's synchronized tremolo look a lot more user-friendly. Since it had the whole decade to make its mark with a new and changing line-up of artists, the 1960s era Stratocaster is perhaps equally popular as its predecessor. Many changes were made to the basic design during the decade, some for the better and some for worse, but you can guarantee that a clean, nicely played-in and playable example from this era will be worth every penny you spend on it!

now incredibly rare, that had a fine piece of mahogany for the body. This added sustain and an interesting figure when finished with a tasty tri-tone sunburst, but these monsters had the disadvantages that they were both incredibly heavy for a Stratocaster and also quite expensive compared to a standard model. Body shapes available varied from a very slim-line body to something relatively thick. It is rare to see a 1960s example in absolutely mint condition, but, if the occasion arises, take time to see how the body compares with that of a reissue or custom shop replica.

The finish on early Stratocasters is nitrocellulose, a thin paint that reacts to sunlight, heat, foam vapours and pretty much anything else. Its unpredictability can have a big influence on a price tag today, while adding to their rarity. This was slightly changed during the CBS era, when Fender added an extra shot of polyurethane to thicken the finish and make it more durable.

## Body

The Stratocaster's body followed the same basic construction as the 1950s model, being cut from either ash or alder and then sanded by hand. These were uncertain times for Fender. Music was changing, tastes were changing and sales of the Stratocaster were falling. During this period Fender began sending out colour charts to dealers, giving full details of all the custom and standard colours available. This was one way for Fender to generate business among players who wouldn't have the nerve to ask the salesman for a colour that they hadn't actually seen. The finish on the Stratocaster's body could be just as varied as it was in the 1950s. There were even a few examples made,

## Neck

The most obvious change in the cosmetics of a 1960s era Stratocaster is the addition of a thick piece of rosewood to the fretboard. Fender's reason for introducing the new design was that dealers had been receiving complaints about the lacquer on the maple fretboard wearing out on early models. Fender solved the problem on the Stratocasters by using rosewood, or sometimes Brazilian rosewood. Gibson had also used rosewood on their Les Paul Standard, which was then out of favour and no longer available from Gibson due to poor sales.

Here is an early 1960s Stratocaster. This particular left-handed model is again an incredibly rare instrument and is in great condition for its age. The wear appears only on the rear of the body, which is very common.

The truss rod was easily fitted underneath the rosewood fretboard before it was added, so that adjustments could be made in the same place as a 1950s model. The guitar's headstock, however, looked even tidier than before as there was now no need for a walnut plug at the top on the neck.

The dot inlays, now made of clay, contrasted well with the dark Brazilian rosewood.

Rosewood fretboards from the earlier 1960s have become known as 'Slab Boards', owing to the thick and easily identifiable slab employed. These early slab board models are now highly sought after. Later in the 1960s the famous slab became a lot thinner, eventually becoming more of a veneer. The wear apparent on 1950s Fender maple fretboards must have caused some concern, so the addition of a thick piece of rosewood was no surprise.

Most Stratocasters from this period feature a shallow C-shape neck and a rosewood fretboard with a good, rounded profile. During the mid-1960s another change happened when CBS bought Fender for $13,000,000. This may seem a large sum by today's standards, but was far more substantial by the standards of 1964–5. The big debate among guitarists and collectors about whether a post-CBS buyout Stratocaster is inferior to the earlier models is often irrelevant, since Fender employees continued working at the factory, making the same guitars as they had weeks before and for few years after. Some of the changes introduced during the 1960s were fine and still appeal today.

The other difference in the Stratocaster from late 1964 is that the logo changed from the 'spaghetti' design to one that was a lot bolder and more easily read, with the 'Fender' logo in gold, outlined in black, and a thin 'Stratocaster'. This was used until early 1968, when the logo was changed again to a thicker 'Fender' and an even thicker 'Stratocaster'.

Stratocaster sales were surprisingly low during the early 1960s, a situation made worse by the imminent British invasion armed with Burns guitars and, most famously, Rickenbackers. Fender's sales teams and ex-

A beautiful Sonic Blue early 60s Stratocaster. This particular example, in its form-fit blonde Tolex case, is finished in one of Fender's most sought-after custom colours. This example also has a wonderful flamed maple neck, which appears sporadically on Stratocasters. The original decal appears to be the only aspect of the guitar that shows wear.

ecutives were on the brink of discontinuing the Stratocaster and inventing newer and trendier models for surf music and promoting such guitars as the Jazz Master and Jaguar. This was until a young man named James Marshall Hendrix adopted a white Stratocaster in 1966 for his own brand of psychedelic blues. At a time when Les Paul guitars were becoming very popular among blues players like Eric Clapton and Mike Bloomfield, the connection with Jimi Hendrix and his debut album, *Are You Experienced* (1967), pretty much saved the Stratocaster. (For a discussion of Jimi Hendrix's Stratocasters and their specifications, *see* Chapter 6.)

Another event of 1966 was that CBS introduced the big headstock. This is like Marmite to most Stratocaster lovers – you either love it or hate it. The big headstock was to remain a feature throughout the 1970s and is now a famous icon for Fender: Jimi Hendrix is mostly seen photographed with CBS models with larger headstocks.

Following the CBS buyout, Fender also changed the dot inlays from clay to pearloid (cheap imitation pearl), which gave the guitars a touch of flair. The most diehard Stratocaster fans, however, have always had an issue that the dots don't line up like the original models from the 1950s. This may be a small concern to some, but it has been an ongoing problem for others.

CBS also advertised in the Stratocaster catalogue that it was available with a bound neck. This was short-lived, but there are a still a few examples of this rare guitar.

## Plastics

Until about 1965 Fender continued to use an early form of plastic that was still a little primitive in longevity and quality, and hence prone to ageing. As a result the majority of plastic parts from original Stratocasters are nowadays usually found to be either cream or mint green, making them easily identifiable when looking at an original guitar.

The newer plastics used from 1965 did not wear as easily, held their colour better and were more durable.

Pickguards on early Stratocasters were three-ply and had eleven screws attaching them to the guitar's body, so keeping the pickguard from warping. Following the buyout, it seems that Fender acquired a cheap supply of pickguard material with one side pearloid and the other plain white, making it perfect for the purpose. On late 1960s Stratocasters it is common to find pearloid underneath where the pickups and electrics are situated.

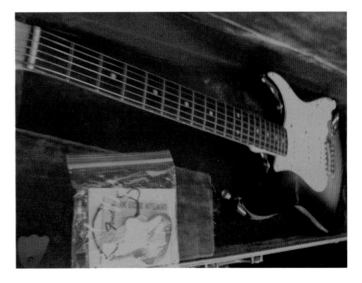

This early 60s Stratocaster is the archetypal 60s model. It features three-tone sunburst with a green nitrate guard, which was replaced by a laminate model later on in the 60s. This specific guitar has all of its features unmarked, with an original case and accessories.

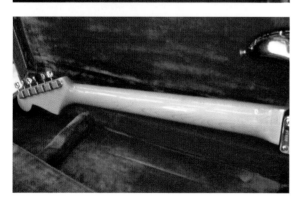

A beautiful 1965 Stratocaster in its new tougher-wearing black tolex case with red interior. These Stratocasters, considered CBS era, are fine instruments but were once considered inferior to a guitar made a matter of weeks earlier. Note the transition logo and amp logo on the case.

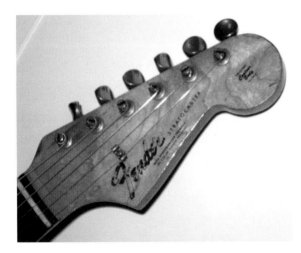

A player's 1965 Stratocaster that has had a heavy life. The guitar is a refinish and shows wear on the transition logo. This is common for '65 Stratocasters, due to the gold in the decal being prone to flaking.

Another custom colour Stratocaster, this time from 1965. This guitar has a slightly faded finish, which only adds to its authenticity. The amount of case accessories on show mean that this guitar has been well cared for and played very little. Note the custom colour chart, rarely seen with a Stratocaster.

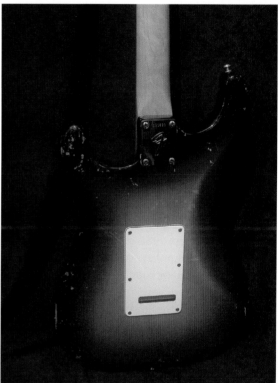

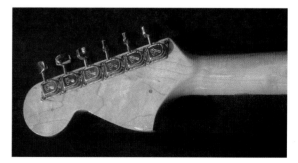

A clean 1969 sunburst Stratocaster. This is the type of Stratocaster that didn't get its full potential value until the early 2000s. Many players believed big headstock guitars were all of poor quality in relation to their early 60s counterparts. It seems odd that no one noticed Jimi Hendrix's extensive use of late 60s Stratocasters. They worked well enough for him on numerous gigs, including Woodstock.

## Electrics

The Stratocaster's electrics changed very little during the early 1960s, but following the mid-1960s buyout plastic-coated wire, which was cheap and readily available, was introduced to save on costs. This was part of the CBS sales ethos of 'make it ours' and 'make it cheap and sell at a huge profit'. Debate on which guitars were better has tended to sway toward older models, owing to their higher manufacturing costs. The mid- to late 1960s guitars have always been cheaper than the earlier models, but they are by no means necessarily worse: Jimi Hendrix and a plethora of other famous players utilized mid- to late 1960s Stratocasters to great success.

Around 1965 Fender would still be making the famous single-coiled Stratocaster pickups, albeit now with a slightly personal touch, perhaps because they had always wanted to or because the material previously used for the bottom of each pickup had not enabled them to do so: the newer models had light grey fibreboard bottoms that allowed whoever created the pickup to sign and date each one with their initials. Pickups from 1965 onwards feature the date, initial and batch number, providing a good way of identifying replaced pickups.

The tonal differences between models from the 1950s and those from the 1960s are as much to do with the pickups as they are the necks. Stratocasters from the 1950s are known for having a much brighter sound than the 1960s models. This is mainly due to rosewood being a slightly softer wood than hard-rock maple.

## Hardware

Throughout the 1960s the same hardware was used as previously, but following the buyout CBS went about patenting a few more things. The backwards 'F', which had been associated with Fender guitars since the company's earliest days, was now patented by CBS and added to all Stratocaster neck plates as a great symbol of the CBS takeover. The name 'Stratocaster' was also patented by CBS.

With all neck plates now sporting the Fender 'F', CBS also changed the tuners in 1968 from the mainstay Klusons to Schaller models. The new Schaller tuners were of similar character to the previous models, apart from the shape and mounting screws. The new tuners featured an 'F' stamp on the rear. Schaller tuners were used for many years on the Stratocaster.

## Cases

Fender had abandoned the tweed case by the early 1960s and replaced it with a case covered with very smart brown Tolex, a material made by the General Tire and Rubber Company; the Stratocaster was now fitting perfectly into the 1960s. This was replaced again in 1963 by a smarter looking blonde model with a green leather trim. These usually have a red plush lining, although reissue cases have black interior.

The cases became even trendier in 1965 when they were completely covered in black Tolex and had a vibrant orange interior; the case ends were black with a white piped trim. Later in the 1960s these also featured a very cool 'amp logo', which made them probably the best and most widely recognized Fender cases after the famous tweed examples.

A 1960s era Fender Stratocaster is a remarkable instrument that connects Hank Marvin, Jimi Hendrix, John Frusciante, Ritchie Blackmore, David Gilmour, Stevie Ray Vaughan, Dick Dale, Ry Cooder and many, many more. It is a cherished instrument in the Fender family and probably the definitive design. The guitar had changed cosmetically but remained an icon. Not many guitars from the 1960s are as popular today.

**OPPOSITE AND OVERLEAF: A complete overview of a 1965 custom colour Stratocaster. This model shows a little wear to the rear of the body and neck and a transition logo placed forward on the guitar; many 1965 Stratocasters had the logo placed here for reasons unknown. They do fit lower down the head stock. The guitar is in 100 per cent original condition and also has its original blonde Tolex case, strap and polishing cloth. Note the grey bottom pickups.**

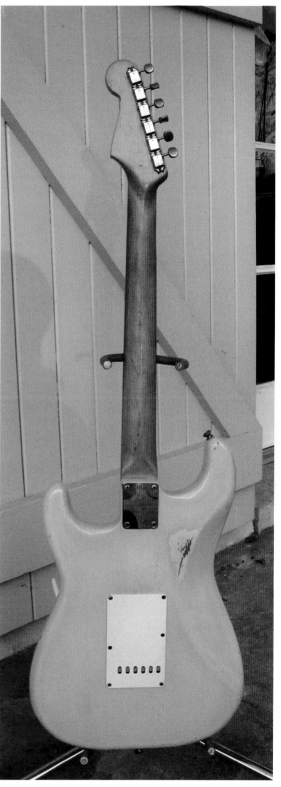

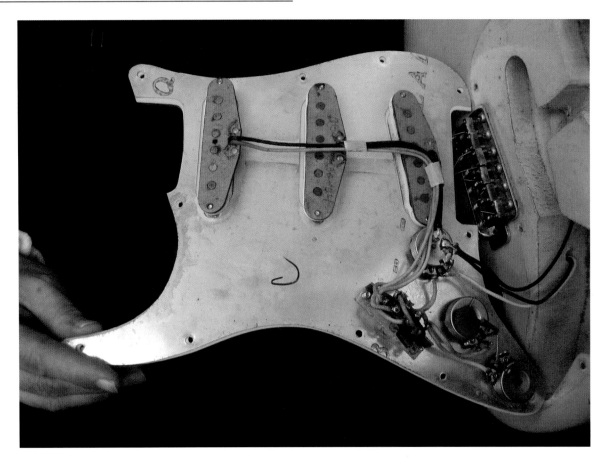

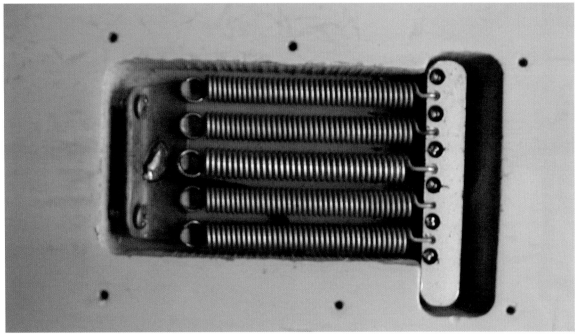

# JIMI HENDRIX STRATOCASTERS

No other guitar player on the face of the earth has had as much impact on the electric guitar and the Fender Stratocaster as one James Marshall Hendrix. His control and diversity as a musician is still revered worldwide, even thirty-eight years after his death. Many players aspire to be him, to sound like him or to learn the songs he created and which have stood the test of time. Jimi was born on 27 November 1942. He began to make his way in the music industry as a backing musician with the Isley Brothers and Little Richard, among others, but was usually sacked from such bands for being too flamboyant and overshadowing the front men by playing the guitar with his teeth or behind his head. Early in 1966 Jimi formed his own group known as Jimmy James and the Blue Flames in New York. Here he was spotted by Chas Chandler of the Animals and was swiftly bought to the UK, where later that year he put together The Jimi Hendrix Experience. This is when things took off. Armed with a white Stratocaster, Jimi wowed audiences with his own brand of electric blues, which had previously only been heard from the likes of Cream and The Rolling Stones. Jimi's musical direction changed from time to time but one thing remained – his innovatory use of any Fender Stratocaster that ended up in his hands.

It is known that Hendrix was prone to buying the latest and greatest effects unit he encountered in his local music shop (usually Manny's Music, New York). In just a few years he got through numerous Stratocasters, many of which were never documented. The guitars he used would never be too far from being stock: he had a habit of buying Stratocasters and then smashing them, giving them away or getting them stolen. Jimi's interesting career is otherwise well documented, resulting in only four albums officially released and just four years of fame.

Jimi Hendrix was pronounced dead on 18 September 1970, following an overdose of sleeping pills and red wine. It was not a suicide or a cry for help, just an accident that cost the world its greatest electric guitar player.

In 1966 Fender/CBS had been on the brink of discontinuing the Stratocaster model from its range due to poor sales, and there are rumours that Jimi's extensive use of the type is the only reason the Stratocaster is alive and kicking today. Jimi's Stratocasters were pretty much always stock, apart from the paint jobs aside. He would turn the Stratocaster upside down to accommodate his left-handed playing, and he would relocate the strap button to the lower body horn and reverse the nut to take his strings. The guitars would be set with a medium to high action with either 9 or 10 gauge strings. The tremolo would usually be set flat against the body with five springs set medium.

The guitars Jimi is usually associated with are the large headstock, late 1960s models, which to many collectors are worth a lot more due to the iconic images of Jimi using them. Jimi is known to have used many Stratocasters throughout his career and, not being a man to stick to one guitar for too long, he would give them away or destroy them. Documenting Jimi's Stratocasters is not an easy job when they may have been lost in spectacular fashion.

## Fender Stratocaster, 1968, Olympic White, Maple Neck (#240981)

This guitar is the iconic 'Woodstock' Stratocaster. It first appeared in Jimi's hands around October 1968 and was used until his death in 1970. This is perhaps the guitar most closely associated with Jimi due to the 'Star Spangled Banner' rendition he soared through at Woodstock in August 1969. The guitar bears the serial number 240981 and was a firm favourite. It appeared at many concerts after its purchase from Manny's Music Store in New York. The guitar is the archetypal late 1960s Stratocaster, featuring an alder body with a nitrocellulose and polyester mix finish that preserves the sheen of a Stratocaster more so than earlier models. The neck features a maple-capped fretboard. To this day it is in good shape and shows few signs of wear and tear.

After Jimi's death it ended up with his drummer Mitch Mitchell, who gave the guitar to Neville Marten in the late 1980s to 'set it up' and clip all the original strings off the guitar. It was then auctioned off by Mitchell at Sotheby's in 1990 to an Italian talk show host named Gabriele Ansaloni for £198,000. Unsubstantiated rumours claim that Ansaloni had originally bid in Italian Lire and was not aware of the high exchange rate. The guitar remained in Ansaloni's possession for three years until it was sold by private sale to Paul Allen, a co-founder of Microsoft. It is known that Allen bought a business class plane seat so that Jimi's guitar could ride back to the States in style. The guitar is now housed at the Experience Music Project/Science Fiction Museum (EMP/SFM) in Seattle, which was also the brainchild of Paul Allen. The museum features hundreds of Jimi Hendrix artefacts, including clothes, pedals, vinyl recordings and literature. The white Stratocaster is the main gem of the collection. It sits on a tall display in front of a wall of Jimi's Marshall amplifiers and still has its 'Ace' guitar strap hovering above it. There has been speculation among Hendrix enthusiasts worldwide that the white Stratocaster in the EMP/SFM is not the one used at Woodstock but an identical model used by Jimi throughout his last European tour. After viewing the footage of Woodstock and the guitar itself, one specific detail confirmed all I needed for my own judgement: on the guitar's headstock you will notice that it has a string tree in line with the F in the Fender decal; this is slightly odd in that Stratocasters from this period usually have the string tree in line with the N in Fender. Rumours will always abound wherever Jimi is concerned.

In 2002 the Fender Custom Shop made four identical clones of the Woodstock Stratocaster with Custom Shop master builders inspecting and photographing the original to get an accurate idea of what was needed, while the output of the pickups was measured to replicate the guitar's volume electrically. Only one of these was made available to the public, when it was sold at the Cooper-Owen auction house in May 2003 for about £15,000. Another was kept by Fender, one went to Experience Hendrix LLC and the last was donated to the EMP museum for allowing permission to access the original.

## Fender Stratocaster, 1968, Black, Maple Neck (#222625)

This is the Stratocaster that Hendrix fans around the world would give almost anything to view: the guitar on which he composed 'The story of life' on the night he died. This was reportedly Jimi's favourite guitar. He nicknamed it 'Black Beauty' and it travelled everywhere with him up until his death. The guitar is identical to the white Woodstock model apart from the finish. Whether there is much difference in playability is unknown as the two of them haven't been seen together since Jimi's last gig at the Isle of Fehmarn festival in Germany on 6 September 1970. The guitar is in slightly worse condition than its white brother, as is shown in photographs that Monika Dannemann (Jimi's last girlfriend) allowed to be taken for issue 10 of *Univibes* magazine. These show wear on the body and neck, as well as a missing adjuster screw and spring for the low E string, which is in the accessory pocket of the case. The lower strap button has come loose and is secured with some green electrical tape. The body shows signs of being hit with Jimi's large rings on the upper body horn as well as small dings all over the body and rear surface scratches. The truss rod adjustment gap at the base of the neck on the pickguard has been made slightly larger for reasons unknown. Apart from two known appearances – for *Univibes* and once for *Guitarist* magazine in 1995 – this guitar has been in hibernation since 1970. The guitar is the Holy Grail for most as it was used in various concerts, including the infamous Band of Gypsys gig at Fillmore East, New York, and the Atlanta pop festival in 1970. The rear of the guitar has some sticky label residue on the neck plate, which is believed to be from peeling away the old price sticker. The black Stratocaster is believed to have been in the possession of the Dannemann family since her death in 1996, and as of 2008 it has still not surfaced in the media or in auction houses.

## Fender Stratocaster, 1965, Fiesta Red (# N/A)

Rumours are constantly going round regarding this guitar, known as the Monterey Stratocaster. It is the guitar, painted half white with psychedelic designs, that Jimi played, burned and finally smashed at the 1967 Monterey Pop Festival in San Francisco. The famous photographs depict Jimi kneeling before it in flames during a frenzied version of 'Wild Thing', which was intended as a combination of the English and American anthems (an English song played by an American). The guitar was bought by Jimi and painted the day before the show as a sacrificial arte-fact. The specifications on Jimi's guitars never really differed from one Stratocaster to the next and this model was no exception, aside from the paint job. The guitar served a few songs in the Experience's de-but US set. With the climax Jimi did an excellent job of upstaging The Who following a backstage disagree-ment as to whether the Experience or The Who would

be first on stage. The guitar suffered the worst: the remaining pieces were thrown out into the audience. From what is known only one piece has surfaced, the bottom right hand section of the body, which is now also housed at the EMP/SFM. Apparently the neck was caught by a journalist who had a front row seat at the festival. The neck then lived on top of the journalist's filing cabinet before being thrown away with various other items as garbage. It has probably since been de-stroyed.

The guitar used at Monterey was recreated by Fender for another Custom Shop release in 1997. The replicas featured hand-painted reproduction designs identical to Jimi's own done by Pamelina H. The gui-tar also came complete with a full ATA rated flight case, suede and fringed gig bag with surf green in-terior, a medley of certificates and paperwork, suede strap, coiled lead and a tongue-in-cheek tin of lighter fluid. At a retail price of around £5,000 there won't be many tins empty or replicas torched! The guitar was also limited to a maximum run of 210. John Mayer is reported to own the prototype of this guitar.

## Fender Stratocaster, 1968, Three-Tone Sunburst (#N/A)

This is the guitar burned by Jimi at the Miami pop festival in 1968. There is very little documentation of this guitar despite its current owner (Dweezil Zappa) restoring the guitar to a playable but by no means original state. The guitar suffered a Hendrix torching to the extent of losing much of its finish. The guitar is reportedly stamped DEMO on the body cavities, indicating that the guitar would have been an artist endorsee model listed by Fender so as not to leave the factory for sale. The guitar would have had all the 1968 appointments, including a large headstock with transition logo. This is a feature on early 1968 Stratocasters before the logo was changed in mid-1968.

The Zappa connection came about when Jimi gave the relic to Frank Zappa following the gig and

Frank briefly used it after heavily modifying it. The guitar now remains in the possession of Frank's son, Dweezil. The guitar is slowly becoming iconic due to the high prices achieved elsewhere and the occasional attempt at a sale from Dweezil. His last asking price was somewhere in the region of £500,000. It failed to sell.

The guitar now hosts a tortoiseshell pickguard, gold hardware, aftermarket pickups and a left-handed maple neck (the guitar would have more than likely been fitted with a rosewood neck). The other interesting feature of this guitar is that it now has a spaghetti logo on the headstock when it would originally have had a bolder CBS logo. This is the least desired of all Hendrix-related Stratocasters.

## Fender Stratocaster, Early 1964, Black (# N/A)

This was the first guitar used during Jimi's set at Monterey (18 June 1967). Its appointments are basically those of a stock, black 1964 Stratocaster, which was also at a gig at Golden Gate Park around the same time. Shortly after it was stolen and the guitar has never been seen since.

There are many great photographs of Jimi using this guitar during the sound check at Monterey and probably playing some of his finest unrecorded work.

## Fender Stratocaster, 1969, Three-Tone Sunburst (#40281)

This Stratocaster was bought by Jimi late in 1969 but seldom used. It is similar to the two favourites used at Woodstock and at the Isle of Wight, but is a three-tone sunburst with a one-piece maple neck. The guitar is identified by its walnut plug, which would indicate a strip down the back of the neck to allow the fitting of a truss rod after the neck construction. The guitar is currently in possession of Richard Friedman, who is one of the third generation of collectors of Hendrix memorabilia. Photographs show it with a brown suede strap similar to the purple one used at the Isle of Wight. This strap is rumoured to have been sold to David Gilmour's wife, Polly Samson, as a sixtieth birthday present for the Pink Floyd guitarist.

## Fender Stratocaster, 1965, Three-Tone Sunburst (#109657)

The Stratocaster bearing the serial number 109657 has only just surfaced after spending the past decades in the possession of Tony Garland. The guitar is reported to have been the very first Fender Stratocaster burned by Jimi, at the Finsbury Astoria, London, in March 1967. Its historical status is enhanced in that it is the guitar on which Jimi played 'Purple Haze' at the Marquee Club (2 March 1967). The guitar these days shows obvious signs of the torching. It has very little finish on the front of the body and little on the rear, and the neck lacquer on the back shows a lot of wear and tear from rings and extensive playing. It must be noted that on 1960s Stratocasters the lacquer on the back of the neck was applied a lot thinner than on other models since the rosewood fingerboards did not require a coat.

There is some speculation about the guitar due to its time spent in a Sussex garage and as to why the guitar has not surfaced before. Since Hendrix Stratocasters sold for well over £100,000 in the early 1990s, Hendrix fans and collectors alike have wondered why the owner did not come forward earlier.

The guitar's electrics and hardware are all part burned, and the pickguard has significantly warped from the heat of the burning lighter fuel. (Following an article in *Guitar and Bass* magazine, this looks like fairly recent scorching.)

In September 2008 the guitar was sold at auction at the Idea Generation Gallery, London, for £280,000.

# Replica and Tribute Model Stratocasters

Jimi Hendrix has been the biggest name for Fender since 1966, when he pretty much saved the Stratocaster from extinction. It seems only fitting that Fender should have a few Stratocasters named after their biggest endorsee, and the company have been looking to produce Stratocasters with some association. The first of these to appear is now known as the Reverse Proto Stratocaster.

### REVERSE PROTO STRATOCASTER
This Stratocaster was billed as the first Jimi Hendrix-related Stratocaster. Originally intended in 1980 as the first type of signature model, the guitar looks similar to the Woodstock model but has a few alterations. The alder body has an extremely odd front contour, known as a 'belly cut', the same as that found on the reverse of the original 1968–69 models. The guitar features a left-handed, one-piece maple neck and usual late 1960s Stratocaster fittings. Problems arose when Fender were denied permission for Jimi's name to be associated with the guitar; the unusual front contour may have been an attempt to get around some form of trademark or likeness issue. Whatever the reason, only four units have been sighted: one went to a collector in Japan, one ended up in the hands of Stevie Ray Vaughan, one appeared in the collection of a Hendrix fanatic in New York, and recently John Mayer has been seen playing the missing prototype. Each model has 'Original Prototype, Not For Resale' inked onto the rear of the headstock. There have been reports that twenty-five prototypes were made, but Fender has confirmed only four.

The guitar that ended up in John Mayer's possession was taken to the Custom Shop in 2005 and inspired the master builder Dennis Galuszka to create 100 replicas for a limited run to be sold worldwide.

### FENDER JIMI HENDRIX TRIBUTE STRATOCASTER
In 1997 Fender and Experience Hendrix LLC, the recently established family estate, finally joined forces

Jimi was a regular customer at Manny's guitar shop in New York. Hence this framed picture, which has been on the wall for many years.

to create a Stratocaster that was a complete tribute to Jimi. The Tribute model that appeared, however, can easily be confused with a Jimi Hendrix Signature Stratocaster but without the signature on the guitar. The model was conceived out of discussions as to how to create a model that everyone can play, but is also a tribute to a great left-handed guitar player who happened to play a Stratocaster upside down. Simple – make a left-handed guitar, period correct to the models Jimi played, and string it upside down to allow the player to 'Experience' what Jimi used himself. The other touch Fender added was to have the logo on the headstock in complete reverse, so that when you stand in front of the mirror with your new Hendrix Tribute Strat you look similar to the man himself. These guitars ran in production for about a year. They were not big sellers but are held in high regard by players and Hendrix fans alike due to the instant cool and the excellent construction. The guitars are basically a mirror image of the famous Woodstock Stratocaster and came complete with a replica ace guitar strap (to a design that Jimi didn't use), a coiled lead like Jimi's and a laser-engraved neck plate bearing Jimi's face, all contained in a period-correct case. These guitars bear serial numbers beginning with TN7.

Here is one of the cleanest and most complete Jimi Hendrix Tribute Stratocasters I have owned. These guitars were introduced in 1997 and became instant collectables.

## FENDER JIMI HENDRIX VOODOO STRATOCASTER

Also in 1997, alongside the tribute model, Fender released the Voodoo Stratocaster for sale to players who weren't comfortable with the left-handed layout. This guitar similarly features Jimi's face on the neck plate and came with the strap, the lead and the correct case. As well as combining a right-handed alder body with a left-handed neck, the bridge pickup was reversed to angle the opposite way. The headstock bears a transition logo. The guitars have Schaller tuners and identical hardware to that on the Tribute model. The model was available with either maple or rosewood fretboard and was available in all the colours Jimi was frequently seen with: black, white or three-tone sunburst. The serial numbers for these guitars also begin with TN7.

## Fenders that Aren't Hendrix Related, but Should Be ...

Since the late 1970s, while Fender have managed to keep the Hendrix Stratocaster in production for only one year, three other models have appeared, under non-Hendrix names, that in their design show obvious signs of his influence or blatant Hendrix connections.

### FENDER '68 REVERSE SPECIAL

This guitar, which appeared at the beginning of 1998, is exactly the same as the Hendrix Voodoo Stratocaster but without the neck plate bearing Jimi's face; it is now engraved 'Fender, Corona, California'. These Stratocasters were also made available in exactly the same colour and neck combinations as the Voodoo model, but they did not come with a Hendrix-style strap or lead. The guitar went out of production in 2002.

### FENDER CUSTOM SHOP '67 REVERSE

This is a rare breed from 1991 that may be viewed as the predecessor of the Voodoo model and the 68' Reverse Special. It has all the same features as its two younger brothers but is built from higher grades of alder for the body and maple for the neck, as well as being fitted with slightly upgraded pickups.

## Legacy

Jimi Hendrix has had quite an impact on Fender's ever growing catalogue. His influence has made many players pick up a guitar for the first time. Having a Hendrix endorsement anywhere on your product will increase sales tenfold. Jimi himself never appeared to care too much about one guitar in particular. They were all expendable. His treatment of Stratocasters is evident on footage taken at Woodstock and the Isle of Wight, where Jimi unstraps his guitar at the end of the gig, drops it to the ground and a dull thud is heard through the PA. Even if you own a guitar with Jimi's name or face on it, or a vintage 1968 Stratocaster with 100w vintage Marshalls and all the vintage effects, this is only half the journey. The guitars and all the paraphernalia do not make the player; only Jimi was able to create the music and it has never been bettered.

## Hendrix on a Budget

It is well known that few Jimi Hendrix fans and collectors can afford to purchase a clean white or black late 1960s Stratocaster. They have pretty much all ended up with collectors or major players; John Mayer, for example, is reported to own both a Woodstock and a Black '68 Stratocaster. With prices for similar Stratocasters bursting through the £20k mark, Hendrix lovers, however, have found that it is still possible to find reissues and signature models (*see* above) at good prices.

It is worth noting that for something approaching the true Hendrix tone the guitar should be one of the types above, especially the 68' Reverse Special, Tribute, Voodoo or Monterey series Stratocasters. Two are particular favourites for achieving the Hendrix tone as it is known.

A unique Jimi Hendrix Custom Shop Stratocaster. This particular guitar is a DIY refinish, hence its unique status.

### FENDER CUSTOM SHOP 1969 STRATOCASTER

This guitar is a definite winner for Hendrix-style playing. Acquiring the guitar in its NOS, Closet Classic or Relic variants will provide you with at least one of the conditions that Jimi used. The guitars are readily available in black, white or sunburst for the Jimi appearance. Maple necks are preferred for the ultimate Jimi experience. These guitars come with Abigail Ybarra hand-wound pickups as standard (pickups bearing her handwritten initial have been found on Jimi's guitars as well as on Buddy Holly's). Second-hand examples of these guitars are readily available and can be considerably cheaper.

### REVERSE PROTO STRATOCASTER

If you should be fortunate to find one, this guitar is a great Hendrix-style Stratocaster with the aged Olympic white finish and a golden maple neck. This guitar also features the famous Abigail Ybarra pickups made

by the Fender Custom Shop. It gives a pretty accurate Hendrix tone as well as appearance. The guitar was produced in a limited edition of 100, which has prevented many players from acquiring one.

Pairing any of the Hendrix Stratocasters with either a Marshall 1959slp Reissue or a 1959HW 100w amplifier will get you somewhere close to the sound you desire.

Effects-wise, it is useful to know that Hendrix's setup rarely differed from having a Fuzz face, Uni-Vibe, octave pedal and wah-wah pedal rigged up at all times. Jim Dunlop has a range of pedals named after Jimi himself and these cover the whole spectrum of Jimi Hendrix sounds. The other options are from mainly boutique guitar effects companies like Voodoo Lab, Sweet Sound or Fox Rox. These companies all make various Jimi Hendrix-influenced effects and have been very successful.

It must also constantly be noted that there was only one Jimi Hendrix. That is all there ever will be.

# 1970s ERA STRATOCASTERS

The 1970s brought tough times for Fender and many other companies as they strove to make guitars to the standards of the previous few years. Fender, now fully owned by CBS, was under pressure to maximize as much revenue as possible from a Stratocaster or Telecaster. Costs of various components were cut down, build quality slipped below the standards of Fender's previous Stratocasters and the guitars quickly fell from grace. Collectors and players alike believe that the high prices and scarcity of vintage instruments is in many ways due to CBS's ownership of Fender and the sub-standard guitars they produced.

The 1970s were the aftermath of the death of hippy culture, free love and unknown dangers of drugs. Times changed, lava lamps arrived and almost everyone had some form of flared trousers. The 1970s was also the decade of Rock – not Rock 'n' Roll but balls to the wall heavy Rock. The tail end of the 1960s saw some of the emerging bands, such as Led Zeppelin, King Crimson, Free and Black Sabbath, begin to appear on TV, radio and supporting big acts. The one thing the majority of these bands had in common was their use of heavyweight Gibson guitars, which, so far as volume goes, have always thrown a strong punch at Fender's single-coil but highly versatile Stratocaster. During the 1970s the Stratocaster had a few names under its belt, notably Ritchie Blackmore of Deep Purple, Jeff Beck, Eric Clapton and Robin Trower. With this brand of blues/technical rock, Fender had a steady stream of guitar players wanting a brand new Stratocaster.

Given all the concern that the 1970s era Stratocaster has caused for many players and collectors, it is perhaps necessary to take some of the rumours about them with a pinch of salt. While the Stratocaster did have a tough time in the 1970s, owing to poor manufacturing, sloppy finishes, three-bolt necks and single-piece tremolos, some 1970s Stratocasters out there are astounding to play and hear. These guitars are now highly priced due to Fender reissues of classic 1970s models in all the classic colours. A notable mention goes to Walter Trout, who rose to fame following his stint with John Mayall's Bluesbreakers (a route earlier taken by Eric Clapton). Trout's use of a 1973, white maple-necked Stratocaster has been an interesting partnership for many years. He bought the guitar new straight off the shelf in Costa Mesa, California, and has very rarely been photographed with another, although admittedly 1973 Stratocasters do have a lot more going for them in the way of quality than a 1979 model possesses.

The general opinion of 1970s Stratocasters is poor. Considering, however, that all the 'good' Stratocasters of 1954 were produced by a team of about 100 people, whereas 1970s Stratocasters were mass-produced to make substantial economies of scale, in the hands of Walter Trout, Robin Trower or Ritchie Blackmore they could still be remarkable instruments. The difference between Fender's production of 268 guitars in 1954 and more than 4,000 in 1979 is quite a jump. There are great 1970s Stratocasters, just as there are 1950s models that in terms of playability and sound are tragically bad. It all depends on taste and patience.

## Body

Most 1970s Stratocasters were made of ash, which is generally a very heavy material but does incorporate a beautiful grain when cut well. The 1970s had everyone clambering after natural wood finishes – cars had wood panels, homes were furnished with wood effect everywhere – and the Stratocaster was no exception. The 1970s era Stratocaster bodies were finished using polyester, which was a first for the guitar industry but did cause consternation among those wanting a nicely resonant, lightweight Stratocaster with a thin coat of paint. The introduction of the polyester finish was a response to complaints from players that their 1950s or 1960s Stratocasters were now looking scruffy, with most of the finish either falling off or completely fading over time. The shiny new polyester finishes were also finished a lot thicker to protect against belt buckles and dings from guitar leads. In the late 1960s Fender experimented with using a thin coat of polyester on top of the nitrocellulose to give extra sheen, but the new 1970s models bodies were completely finished in polyester after CBS realized how much money could be saved using a single mixture of polyester instead of the two coats.

The coat of polyester was bulletproof, but problems arose when players realized how dead their new Stratocasters sounded. The older 1950s and 1960s models seemed to ring more with each note and had a back-saving lightweight construction of hand-carved alder and maple.

While some players took issue with the polyester finish and the tonal differences, the problem that really haunted the 1970s Stratocaster was the neck pocket in the rout in the body itself, which was often cut too large to accommodate the neck. Since the finish was so thick it needed a lot more room to settle and to avoid unsightly cracks appearing around the pocket once a neck was installed. While adding room to the neck pocket was the biggest downfall, Fender had also done away with the classic four-bolt neck construction and replaced it with a shield-shaped, 'F'-stamped three-bolt version with a micro-tilt system that would alleviate the need for a shim to be added for correct neck height. The new three-bolt system seen on the rear of 1970s Stratocasters was introduced around 1972, the year that many customers believe marked the start of a monumental slide in production quality. The new three-bolt neck, set in its larger-than-life neck pocket in the body, allowed the neck to move to the left or right whenever the player picked it up or put it down, knocking all the strings out of tune. Once started this type of wear soon became worse.

One way of remedying the problem came when players and guitar builders began to take their Stratocaster apart and drill another neck screw into the body underneath the neck plate to look neater. Many even tried to convert their Stratocasters back to four-bolt necks, but with little success. Even five bolts in the neck would have made little difference. The source of all neck movement was, and always will be, a badly routed neck pocket and many guitar players began stuffing whatever they could find into the neck pocket in an attempt to fix the ongoing issue.

During the late 1970s Fender spiced up the range by using brighter, obscure colours for their 'International' series, which would incorporate such finishes as Capri Orange and Maui Blue. The finishes on these guitars are usually as thick as on previous models but less sloppy in parts.

Towards the end of the 1970s the finish on Fender guitars became, if anything, slightly worse, as players noticed that the paint on new Stratocasters had a slightly 'orange peel' texture, showing that not enough care had been taken in drying at the factory, or there were ripples in the overall finish. This is about the time when players began hunting for Stratocasters from the 1950s or 1960s, since 'old' Stratocasters could be had for less than half the price of a new one.

OPPOSITE AND OVERLEAF: Here is a clean yet modified 1975 Stratocaster. This model is in the style of the times, and the 1970s trend for guitars was to have as much wood on show as possible. This is how many 1970s Stratocasters looked, with ash body and maple neck, with either white or black plastics. This specific guitar has had some of its electrics changed to newer Japanese units; however, the rest of the guitar remains original.

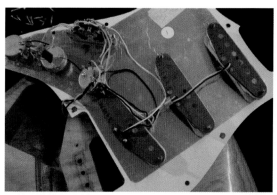

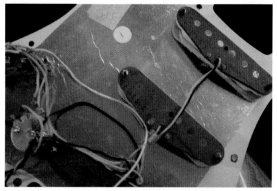

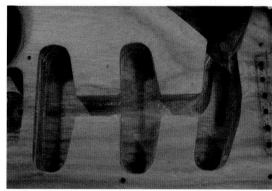

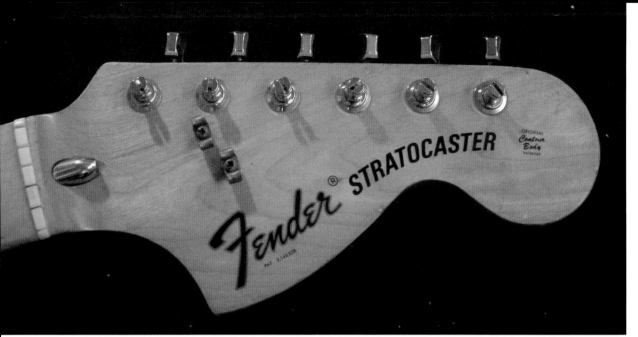

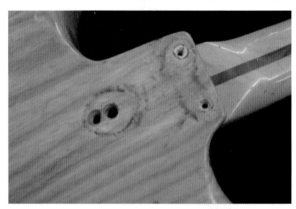

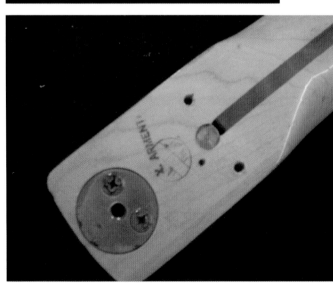

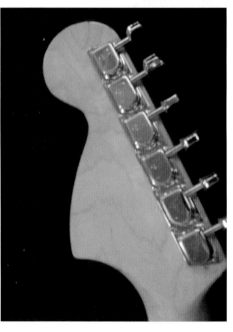

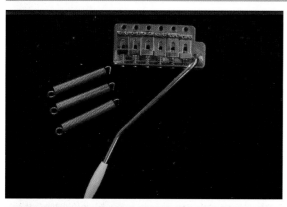

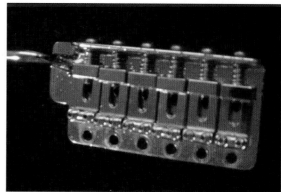

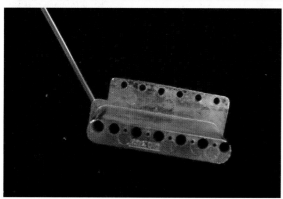

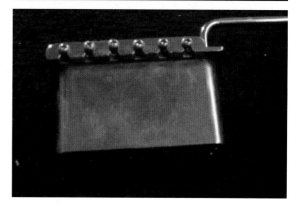

## Neck

Stratocaster necks from the 1970s are by no means lacking in quality, except that many feel that the newly designed truss rod adjustment that Fender incorporated in Stratocasters from 1972 was unsightly. The necks were finished with the same polyester as the body. There is one slight difference, though, as the headstock was oversprayed with nitrocellulose. Nowadays 1970s Stratocasters sometimes look peculiar since the headstock front has aged a lot more than the rest of the guitar; they seem to vary from a very light gold colour to almost brown on the headstock front, sometimes even overshadowing the decal. The other oddball feature about a 1970s era Stratocaster was the addition of the two string trees in late 1973. The headstock now looked more cluttered than on previous years' models.

The decal went through further changes after its first move away from the transitional logo, which looked out of place on the new larger headstock brought in from 1967. Over time many players came to warm to this; the exceptions, of course, are the Hendrix fanatics who have always loved the larger headstock.

The truss rod adjustment, on the other hand, has never been popular with collectors. It is known as 'the bullet', as it resembles a silver bullet sticking out from the base of the headstock. The truss rod itself is identical to that of earlier models except for the instantly identifiable bullet, which alleviated the need to remove the neck to adjust the trueness. It was now possible for the player to grab an Allen key and adjust the guitar with the neck 'firmly' attached to the body and all six strings still in their respective places.

As polyester is a thick finish, it dries a lot harder than nitrocellulose. Fender seemingly thought that the maple neck varieties of 1970s Stratocasters would last for years and years and always have a pristine looking neck to match the body. Unfortunately as soon as the slightest bit of wear appeared, the finish would come off in large splinters and chunks, leaving bright, unfinished wood underneath, against which the tinted lacquer would look quite strange.

A friend of mine named JC owns a 1979 International series Stratocaster in Maui Blue, complete with a hated glossy polyester finish on the maple neck, which his parents bought for him in Northern Ireland. He told me how he once tried to strip the varnish off the back of the neck and described the clear varnish when removed as being like shards of glass. This suggests that the polyester coat had not really stuck to the wood, unlike nitrocellulose, and that the polyester had clung to the neck for years and then had to pulled off rather than stripped.

It is quite common today to see necks that have been worn down to the wood on the edges. This is not as common on rosewood-necked models, since polyester was not applied to the rear of the neck. Rosewood models from this period tend to be more sought after.

The dot inlays in the fretboards of 1970s Stratocaster necks tend to be put in at slightly odd places. The famous point of recognition for dot inlays is at the twelfth fret, where they should both line up neatly with the A string and the B string. Most 1970s Stratocasters, however, have done away with that rule and the dots are usually under the A string and line up perfectly with the B string or vice versa. This, although only a cosmetic feature, made some players worry as to what was going on at the Fender factory.

The radius of 1970s necks could vary greatly: your new Stratocaster may have had an enormous neck, but the one hanging next to it may have been the thinnest you had ever played. There was too little consistency for most players' liking. Shops taking ten or fifteen instruments would sometimes find themselves left with four heavyweight, large-necked, poorly finished Stratocasters that no-one wanted and they would need to offer at a heavy discount to achieve a sale.

Frets added to the Stratocaster were usually inserted as well as they had always been and finished nicely at the edges too. Players had another gripe, however, since many Stratocasters from this period suffered from having poorly cut nuts, and shops resorted to replacing them when the guitars arrived. My father recalls being in a guitar shop in Luton in the late 1970s and watching them box up brand new Stratocasters to be sent back to Fender due to poor manufacturing. This was common but some shops either wouldn't or couldn't carry out the job themselves – but then again, why should they?

## Hardware

One of Fender's biggest mistakes on the 1970s Stratocaster was to do away with the two-piece vibrato, which had become so accepted in modern music and playing styles, and replace it with a single cast unit that players could not separate should they need to. The 1970s cast unit bridge was not as massive as previous models and had noticeable tonal differences: there is, for instance, little sustain from a cast bridge. Fender's thinking may have been rational in that, since most players never needed to take the tremolo apart, why not make a one-piece cast version? Well, given the tremolo arm system Fender had been using for some time, there had always been heavy-handed players who are able to snap the tremolo arm in the block. This includes me. Snapped tremolo arms in a two-piece tremolo system are an easy fix since the bridge plate is connected to the block by just three short countersunk screws: undo these, drill out the old arm, replace the thread and add a new tremolo arm; failing that, buy a new block at small expense and bolt to the plate with three screws, with the new arm already in. Job done. Should you snap the arm in a cast unit, however, it's back to Fender for a completely new unit, plate, saddles, block, saddle screws and arm. The 1970s tremolo systems are not as economical for the player but were a big saving on the manufacturing costs – another few dollars for the CBS management.

The saddles on the 1970s Stratocaster were altered to look slightly more 'blocky' than the previous models. These also had a small part number stamped underneath each saddle. Fender had the idea of making the Stratocaster saddles neater with thicker-looking units than before; they succeeded, but it's just a shame about the rest of the bridge set-up.

The machine heads on the 1970s era Stratocaster stayed the same as they had been since the Schaller models arrived in 1968. They did the job as well as the earlier Kluson models, but the infamous Fender 'F' stamped onto the rear casing made the guitars' identity the most blatant it had ever been.

## Electrics and Plastics

The electrics found on 1970s era Stratocasters have often been altered or replaced due to the many alterations inflicted on them, although the pots and switches on 70s Stratocaster guitars remained of pretty high quality, using CTS pots and CRL switches throughout. One let-down discovered by players at the time was that Fender had switched from using cloth-covered wire, which always made the player feel his guitar was wired with due care and attention, to plastic-coated wire, which is always cheaper than cloth-covered varieties. The orange Sprague capacitor remained in place throughout the 1970s electrics.

The other breakthrough for the 1970s Stratocaster is the five-way switch. For years players had relied on jamming cardboard in their three-way switches to create the famous out-of-phase sounds of the neck and middle, and of the middle and bridge pickups. Now CRL had finally come up with a five-way model that would sit in these positions.

Pickups were also a sticky point for players as the guitars were now fitted with flush pole piece pickups. These looked slightly odd on the Stratocaster, which for years had been known for its staggered pole pieces, adding an awful lot of tone to the individual string for which the pole piece worked. The B and E string on a 1950s or 1960s Stratocaster, for example, is lower than the others to take the shrill highs out of the pickup and balance the four other pole pieces to create an even sound. It is also known that Fender thought that string technology of the 1970s rendered staggered pole pieces irrelevant. During the 1970s Stratocaster pickups were flush with each other, which gave a flat overall sound without much tonal difference. The combination of the flush pickups, the thick polyester finish and the cast bridge unit all added up to very flat and dull sounding guitars.

Plastics used on 1970s era Stratocasters were not very different to those in the previous models and have lasted well compared to the Bakelite units from the early 1950s or nitrate 1960s guards.

The international series Stratocasters came with white pickguards complete with black pickup covers and knobs. This was the beginning of the 1970s black plastic revolution and at one point many Stratocasters left the factory with completely black plastics, depending on the finish: darker colours, such as mocha brown, were offset with black plastics.

One slight difference was that Fender now used a plain white sticker branded with the Fender logo as well as the specific guitar's serial number printed on it in black ink. It is not known when Fender decided to start this feature but it may have been introduced in the late 1970s, supposedly to give more brand recognition as well as to stop the fakes that had slowly started to appear from offshore manufacturers in Italy, Japan and elsewhere.

## Case and Reissues

The cases used by Fender for the 1970s Stratocaster had the same black Tolex with plush red lining as in the late 1960s, although throughout the 1970s this became progressively lighter until it reached a brilliant orange colour.

It always seemed most unlikely that the 1970s Stratocaster would ever be reissued, but in 2006 Fender did the unthinkable and reissued a 1970s model, available in white, black, sunburst or natural (obviously!), and in either rosewood or maple. It is not an accurate reissue, but instead Fender have made a guitar that incorporates the best features of the 1970s style Stratocaster, although weirdly enough this still leaves it some way from the original model.

The saddles on the reissue are vintage-style, bent-steel units. Thankfully the bridge is of the two-piece type and the tuners are still Schaller. One unfortunate snag is that if you attempt to restring a reissue Stratocaster with anything heavier than a 46.gauge E string it will not fit and requires drilling out, since the string end will not go in the anchor hole; original 1970s models, however, took most gauges.

The 1970s era model has its own qualities but is still a Stratocaster. Take note of everything you've heard and, if it doesn't float your boat, look elsewhere as it can be a difficult guitar. They are heavy, but in the right hands they are loved and cherished just like those from the 1950s and 1960s.

# THE JAPANESE INVASION

Fender's reputation was in decline in the 1970s under the ownership of CBS, owing to the poor-quality Stratocasters that were in abundance throughout the world's guitar shops. As the 1980s approached, the UK economy was in the doldrums and unemployment was not far from three million. Guitar players in the UK were in urgent need of cheaper alternatives. Enter Tokai.

Tokai Gakki was spawned in 1947 and originally began making parts for Martin guitars to save on costs. The company came into its own in 1976 by creating a Les Paul replica, which was branded with a Gibson-styled Tokai logo on the headstock tip with 'Les Paul Reborn' (as opposed to Gibson's 'Les Paul Model') in the same font and colour. This 'near the knuckle' feature caught the attention of many customers and sold incredibly well due to its high-end construction and knockout price. The new 'Reborn' Les Pauls were soon followed by a Stratocaster.

Players the world over had begun to apply the term 'Pre-CBS' to the best Fender Stratocasters, with small headstocks, thin finishes, great tone and fantastic playability. Word got back to Tokai following their 'Reborn' model that there was a huge market for old-style Stratocasters. With Eric Clapton and many others playing 'Pre-CBS' guitars, it seemed inevitable that Tokai would meet the demand.

The first Tokais appeared in 1977. Tokai had sought out great 1950s and 1960s Stratocasters from Billy Gibbons, Joe Walsh and Rick Nielsen, who were known for their unique tones when playing and their extensive guitar collections. Tokai asked for permission to dismantle and examine their finest Stratocasters, measurements were taken and outputs were read. Prototypes were tested and the first Tokai Stratocasters then went into production, under Fender's radar.

## Body

The First Tokai Stratocasters used high-quality wood for the bodies; as with Fender, there was an option for ash. Tokai had the advantage over Fender, hobbled by CBS's insistence on keeping costs low and using cheaper wood, that Japan had not yet signed the Convention on International Trade in Endangered Species (CITES), which prohibited the use of Brazilian rosewood and other rare woods. The USA signed up in 1974, and Japan followed in 1980. The bodies of early Tokai Stratocasters were well shaped, more akin to early Stratocasters. They seemed to have all the right features, thinner bodies, thinner paint and light weight. They were usually constructed in either one or two pieces of alder or ash and generally had attractive grains.

Tokai also took note of players' needs by adding custom colours to the bodies: metallic green, black and natural. The new guitars' bodies had all the right routing, and underneath the pickguard you will find neat and clean channel routs for all three pickups and the famous extra wiring channel. The bodies also managed to give a fantastic tone too, making these guitars scarily good to many players in the UK when the invasion arrived.

During Tokai's heyday in the 1980s, the company even made a seriously tongue-in-cheek poke at Fender by replicating a 1970s era original. The new guitars had the same body construction, using ash, and observed all the finishes and cosmetics that had been so unsuccessful for Fender. The '1970s' Tokai bodies, however, were much better made than the average 1970s Stratocaster, the finishes weren't sloppy, the weight was much easier going on the player's shoulder and the shape of the horns and contours were a lot more pleasing to the eye, following the Stratocaster shape more closely than Fender did in the 1970s.

## Necks

The early Tokais were available in either maple or rosewood (following Fender). The only blot that Tokai made to its copybook was to add a separate 'skunk stripe', as seen on early 1950s Stratocasters until a separate rosewood fretboard was added, so eliminating the need for a separate channel on the back of the neck for the truss rod to be fitted. The mistake was obviously pointed out to Tokai, who phased it out in future replicas. The rosewood-necked versions were fitted with a perfect 'slab board', which is a favourite feature for many guitar players.

The cosmetics of the neck included white plastic dots on the rosewood-necked models and black plastic dots in the correct places on the maple-neck models, as well as pearloid dot markers. The 1970s style Tokais came complete with the dreaded 'bullet' truss rod adjuster at the bottom of the headstock and the three-bolt neck join with the micro-tilt built in; whereas Fender had stamped the three-bolt plates, on the Tokai models these were left blank.

## Headstocks

Probably the most notorious memory of the Tokai 'Stratocasters' is the dicing-with-death brand names that Tokai applied to the new guitars.

On early models Tokai basically took a Fender 1950s Stratocaster headstock decal and shaped it using the same fonts and colours to create their 'own' decal that would fool anyone from five feet away. It didn't technically read 'Tokai', but was more like 'Fokai', incorporating the 'F' from the famous spaghetti logo.

Shortly after the appearance of these guitars Fender and Gibson noticed that sales of their own models were slipping. In 1982 they reacted by creating their own sub-brands, which could forcefully recover the market from Tokai by adding their own names and replicating their own models. This was a guaranteed winner with many guitar players.

Tokai were served with a lawsuit from Fender. Under pressure to change the branding on the replicas, a different decal was applied for the UK market that did away with any Fender similarities and just read TOKAI in a plain black, bold font. Tokais were advertised in the UK by showing a friend of the distributor holding a Tokai and saying 'Tokai is coming'; the distributor was Blue Suede Music, who began importing Tokais into the UK in 1982.

For the US market Tokai reshaped the headstock on their Stratocasters to avoid Fender slamming the law down on them once again.

| ORIGINAL DECAL USED BY FENDER STRATOCASTER, 1954–69 | FIRST AND '1970S' DECAL USED BY TOKAI ON EARLY REPLICA STRATOCASTERS, 1982 |
| --- | --- |
| Fender Stratocaster | Tokai Springy Sound |
| Tokai Silver Star (1970s) | (NB mid–late 1970s Fenders only had the 'Fender Stratocaster' decal) |
| With Synchronized Tremolo | This is the exact replica of a good old Strat |
| Original Contour Body | Oldies But Goldies |

The bold TOKAI logo remained on the guitars in 1983 until the heat from Fender and Gibson had cooled and Tokai could find a new logo that didn't tread too hard on the Americans' toes. They came up with a pseudo-transition logo that combined the spaghetti logo and the 1965 Fender 'Transition' logo from the CBS buyout era. The logo was then changed yet again:

| ORIGINAL DECAL USED BY FENDER ON THE STRATOCASTER, 1954–69 | THIRD DECAL USED BY TOKAI FOLLOWING THE LAWSUIT AND THE BOLD TOKAI LOGO |
| --- | --- |
| Fender Stratocaster | Tokai Goldstar Sound |

This logo has remained to the present day. The newer Tokais have reshaped headstocks similar to those introduced in the lawsuit era.

## Hardware

The hardware used on Tokai Goldstars, Springy Sounds and Silver Stars was copied from the Fender originals of their respective years. Where Fenders would read 'PAT. PEND', Tokai cheekily opted for 'FINAL PAT. PEND' – guaranteed to enrage Fender even more. The Silver Star featured cast block-style saddles identical to 1970s Fenders.

The tuners on the Tokai Stratocasters were usually found to be great sounding Japanese-made Kluson replicas that were identical down to the hole in the string post that accommodated loose string ends. For some reason the tuner on the Silver Star was not identical to that of a 1970s Stratocaster: it retained the offset diamond-shaped casing and tuning key, but differences are noticeable in the non-split string post and hole for loose ends.

## Electrics

Many Tokais have small and cheap electrics, although some models classed at the top end feature heavy-duty switches and pots, all hooked up with the cloth-covered wire that Fender had formerly been associated with. The pickups, however, proved many players wrong by being extremely good at providing scarily Stratocaster-like tones. The majority of Tokais found today usually have the original electrics removed and replaced with aftermarket parts.

## Value for Money

In many ways Tokai Stratocasters were the first reissues and provided a cheap Stratocaster, manufactured to the build ethic of the early models, that could be similarly gigged or cherished. The current Tokai Stratocaster is a different animal. It does not hold the same charm as older models, due to Tokai changing the headstock to avoid any recurrence of the lawsuits of the 1980s.

Many guitar players could not believe how good Tokais were for the money. They have been popular since their arrival and will be coveted for years to come. There are websites where you can register your Tokai and there is a loyal following that frequently scours guitar shops hoping for a bargain.

This type of desirability has sent prices through the roof for earlier and higher end models. What was once a budget copy has now become a collectable commodity.

It is interesting to note that for many years players would scratch the Tokai logo off the top of their guitar, but since the rise of fraud the world over, players are now seeking makers of Tokai decals to restore their guitars to their former glory.

The Japanese version of the Stratocaster.

## How to Avoid Buying a Fake Fender Stratocaster or Tokai

Fakes are very common and when making a purchase one should look for telltale signs:

- Lacquer, usually car spray paint on the headstock front, will have orange peel effect, bubbles in the finish or runs if done improperly. Generally the work will be sloppy on the front and only rarely carried out on the back of the headstock or neck itself.
- Since the Tokai invasion, numerous other Far Eastern guitars have reached the UK market. These guitars are unusually light and generally come with a blank headstock when new. It is very common for them to acquire a Fender decal at some point. Look out for sloppy lacquer or a dry decal on top of the finish, which will easily scratch off with a light fingernail.

- Most fake guitars have very poor quality machine heads. Check whether the guitar you are thinking of buying has had a machine head change.
- If the neck is bright orange in colour, this is a sign that the guitar was not made by either Fender or Tokai.
- The truss rod adjuster may be large and filled in with wood filler; check that there is an adjuster at the base of the neck, or otherwise how will you adjust your truss rod when the hole is full of brown wood filler?
- The headstock of the guitar should be in one piece. If there are one or two visible lines showing that it is in more than one piece, run like hell.
- Tremolo arms should not have a thread the same diameter as the rest of the arm. This is a sign of very cheap manufacturing and one dive bomb can snap an arm instantly.
- Two string trees? Small headstock? Alarm bells should ring unless the seller has added them himself.

I write these points from experience. I once purchased what I believed to be a genuine 1968 Stratocaster identical to a Woodstock model with maple neck, cream plastics and all. I did some research into it and discovered that my £3,000 investment was actually a cheap Japanese copy with upgraded electrics. This was one mistake that I hope no-one else makes. Taking chances on guitars at this price is not advised.

## I Bought One of Those!

Here are some questions and answers I have collected from a Tokai fan who was there the first time around, waiting with £130 in hand ready to buy Japan's finest guitars.

- Can you remember the first Tokai you bought, where and when?

    *I bought mine in what was later to become Soho Soundhouse in London in around 1984.*

- What were your first thoughts when you saw one hanging up in a guitar store?

    *Well, at first I thought I'd found a mint '50s Strat. I could see the low price and pretty much new I'd be leaving the shop with it!*

- Did you use it live? Did it stand up to other Stratocasters you had played previously?

    *To be honest, at that time those guitars that Fender were making were pretty bad and I had sold my Fender because of it. I used the Tokai live all the time, and it became my number one.*

- Do you still have the guitar?

    *Unfortunately mine was stolen from the back of my car.*

- Did you alter or modify the guitar to your playing tastes?

    *I did nothing to modify it – the guitar was perfect in every way.*

- Are you surprised to know that some Tokais are more expensive than genuine Fenders from the 1980s?

    *Really? That doesn't surprise me that much – good food for thought, though.*

# COMMON ALTERATIONS TO THE FENDER STRATOCASTER

The Fender Stratocaster has a reputation as a great workhorse guitar that was simply bolted together with easily soldered electrics. It became apparent to players that you could very easily modify a Stratocaster and leave your mint condition '59 Les Paul in original condition.

The first experiments with modifying a Stratocaster can be dated to the early to mid-1970s. Players felt that, for example, they could easily have the best of both worlds by putting a Les Paul pickup in the bridge of their Strat. This type of modification, or 'mod' as it's known, would require the guitar to have its body routed to accept such a pickup and the pickguard would also have to be altered. Such mods are very common on 1970s Stratocasters and occasionally on 1960s models.

The locking bridge or 'Floyd Rose' tremolo system is another mod commonly seen on Stratocasters equipped with humbuckers. The device is particularly useful for heavy metal music; the unit locks the end of the string into the saddle and locks again at the nut. This type of mod is often seen on 1970s Stratocasters. It involves routing the front of the body to accept the unit itself and again a lot of alteration is needed at the nut to install the lock. Back in the 1970s artists started doing this for themselves, setting off a chain reaction with both other players and the parts manufacturers. All of a sudden every company made a pickguard that would accept a humbucker and light strings became very fashionable.

The Floyd Rose system works very well for its purpose: you can 'dive bomb' notes that you would normally sacrifice tuning problems for, and you can bend notes up and not just down. Pair it with a humbucker and you have something perfect for heavy metal. One reason this combination appealed to players was that 1970s Strats weren't of the best quality and parts were not as good as on previous models. This spurred a lot of players to take up a DIY ethic and try to improve their guitars.

Around this time, micro-switching systems came into play. These were tiny switches that could split a humbucker into two parts and give the player even more tones. The Telecaster was probably the first model to be 'bastardized' by players: a humbucker in a Telecaster was a great combination, and such players as Andy Summers and Keith Richards utilized them frequently. Fender went a step further by making Telecaster Thinline, Deluxe and Custom variants from the late 1960s through to 1978. These guitars were made so that players didn't have to tear their Tele to bits. All three had humbuckers, but some had them combined with the original Telecaster pickups.

The Stratocaster remained untouched by professional manufacturing during this time and it was left for the players to do their worst: some of the mods were crudely done with chiselled routing and poor soldering. There are a number of Stratocasters in the current Fender line that feature humbuckers. This is fine because current model Fenders in the standard lines are not worth as much as vintage ones.

Another popular mod added to Fender Stratocasters of this time was locking machine heads. These helped ease the tuning problems that dogged the Fender Stratocaster for many years. The guitar's original tuners could function OK, but more drastic playing techniques and old age would eventually wear out a Kluson machine head. New makes of machine heads began popping up everywhere, including the popular brands Schaller, Grover and Sperzel, and these were relatively easy to fit. They would aid tuning and generally give your guitar a 'cool custom' look – having a customized guitar was as cool as having a Ferrari engine in your Ford Granada.

## Finishes

Few players around this time decided to have their guitar refinished, since it was a great expense and guitars made in the late 1960s and the 1970s were finished in 'bulletproof' polyester paint. Early models, however, are very commonly refinished, either to give the guitar a great 'new' feel or to fit in with current trends (*see* Chapter 4).

I once spoke to a gentleman who had bought a 1960 Stratocaster in the mid-1960s in a beautiful three-tone sunburst. He was a big fan of flying Vs and outlandish colours and decided that this was not the guitar for him. So he cut the body down to a basic V shape and repainted the guitar in fluorescent pink. A rare breed of guitar and a rare breed of player indeed. Needless to say, he has lived to regret this.

The Stratocaster and Telecaster provide plenty of evidence for changing trends in music over the past fifty years. After all the modifications on Fender Stratocasters in the 1970s, for example, the 1980s was the period of Heavy Metal music, which demanded guitars already equipped with locking tremolos, nuts and humbuckers. This made the 1980s a prime time for picking up a complete vintage guitar bargain. Eric Clapton bought a whole rack of 1950s Stratocasters at this time and assembled his famous 'Blackie' Stratocaster out of three of them. This may have been an early mod but it was definitely successful, since it was sold at auction in 2004 for $959,500, a world record sum!

The vintage guitar market was not at its strongest around this time and most players did not even look twice at modified Strats.

Vintage Stratocasters are usually found with various modifications. An early 1950s Stratocaster, for instance, will usually be found with a refinished body. This is common as players at the time demanded shiny

guitars and wanted to show that they took good care of their instrument. More recently guitar players have been seeking worn guitars that appeal to the Stevie Ray Vaughan fans or those who envy Rory Gallagher's battered Stratocaster. Refinished guitars don't appeal as much as a battered old model: a 2cm bit of paint on an original model is worth almost as much as a whole body refinished in new paint.

Another common modification/repair is usually found embedded on the fretboard of an old Stratocaster. Frets wear out, plain and simple. If you have a 1950s car you know that the brakes are probably not the ones it left the factory with. While it may sometimes be difficult to tell, you can be pretty certain from the overall condition of the car and how many miles are on the clock. It's the same principle with a Stratocaster. If there is an old battered Stratocaster hanging up in a shop, and if it plays well, it's almost certainly had a refret.

Electrics are also prime candidates for replacements. The potentiometers and switches are usually replaced due to heavy usage. The dates are printed on the sides and glared at by collectors and investors. Pickups usually stay in working order and in fact get better with age as the magnets weaken and give a lower output, which is often toneful. However, a pickup can also die over the years: if one winding snaps around the coil it'll need rewinding. This is a feature commonly found on vintage Stratocasters and is usually stated by a dealer.

Input jacks are also subject to constant abuse from leads going in and out on a nightly basis. Strangely enough the metals can lose a lot of their conductivity internally and just die or not conduct enough of a signal.

Machine heads take a battering over their lives and the originals have usually given up on well-used 1950s and 1960s models.

On older guitars the nuts have also usually been changed.

The problem that faces many Stratocaster players and collectors is that the majority of guitars have been used throughout their years and are in a used condition. Collectors, on the other hand, are looking for 'museum quality' guitars. These are the untouched

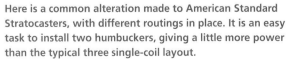

Here is a common alteration made to American Standard Stratocasters, with different routings in place. It is an easy task to install two humbuckers, giving a little more power than the typical three single-coil layout.

examples that still have their shipping carton, strap, lead, manual, hang tags, strings and case. The guitar must be so clean you could enjoy a meal off its body.

Given the scarcity of such guitars, however, it's very uncommon to find them, so the prices of refinished guitars are rising and pushing up the originals even more; I have watched tatty 1960s Stratocasters go from £2,000 to £14,000 in just twelve years.

There will always be a strict divide between players and collectors in guitar terms. A player will happily be like Rory Gallagher and take a battered Stratocaster out of a case and play it for hours every night, whereas a collector will only gaze at his collection with dollar signs in his eyes.

I remember watching an interview with Bonnie Raitt on a 1993 documentary entitled *Curves, Contours and Body Horns*. Regarding the collector/player debate, she put it bluntly, 'It's a tree, honour it'.

Never has a truer word been spoken about Fender Stratocasters.

## Floyd Rose Tremolo

These words can reduce strict Stratocaster purists to tears. The Floyd Rose tremolo system, originally designed back in 1977, is still in production and in use, but seldom by Fender themselves.

Few official instruments have been fitted with the Floyd Rose: two of the best were the Richie Sambora Signature model and the Floyd Rose Classic Stratocaster, These types of Stratocaster were forced out of Fender at a time when Bon Jovi's records were selling in large numbers and the younger generation wanted Stratocasters like Richie Sambora's, fitted with humbuckers and Floyd Rose pickups. The Fender Custom Shop created Sambora's model, while Fender Japan began manufacturing various types of Stratocaster like the ones shown in music videos and used by stadium rock acts.

Fender USA also began to make waves by releasing the Floyd Rose Classic, which incorporated a 1950s style Stratocaster with a Floyd Rose and Dimarzio Pro PAF in the bridge position. The guitar was a moderate

success with the relatively young players at whom the new model was mostly marketed. The guitar was released in 1992 and remained available for a few years. There was also a set neck version that featured flame top maple as well as the ever cool reverse headstock. The cool factor of these guitars was short-lived since most players did not favour straying from the original Stratocaster design.

The Stratocasters that did not survive the 1970s Floyd Rose fashion can usually be found at very little expense since the mods were often done improperly. Those that were done with due care can still be good guitars, but approach them with caution if a purchase is being made. Once a decent Stratocaster has had a Floyd fitted, it's game over until a like-minded player seeks a second-hand one.

## The Humbucker

There has always been a divide between Stratocaster fans over this modification. When connected to a vintage instrument it is just as great a sacrilege as the Floyd Rose. It is not worth modifying a vintage Stratocaster in this way unless you will only ever use the one Stratocaster and have a really good idea of the humbucker's sound in your head.

Many players tend to get humbuckers installed to replicate Gibson tones, but what is usually forgotten is there is a lot more wood and less plastic on a Les Paul, and this is heard in the overall sound.

A modern Stratocaster with humbuckers fitted can be a useful instrument, though. Knowing that on an American Standard, for example, you can build a separate pickguard on which you can have either humbuckers or single-coil configurations at any moment, with just a few solder joints, makes it a perfect workhorse guitar in many players' eyes. The common configurations are either HH (Humbucker-Humbucker) or HSS (Humbucker Single Coil-Single Coil).

Humbuckers are also useful by being coil tap-able; this means you can switch half of the humbucker off for single-coil use – a useful invention.

# MY FENDER STRATOCASTERS

I have had my share of Stratocasters. One of the advantages of working in guitar shops for many years is that I have sometimes been lucky to pick them up for less than others have to pay. I thought it might be worth following the course of my Stratocaster experience by describing the most memorable instruments I have owned, how I ended up with each and what I eventually did with them – sold, modified, traded, smashed to bits ...

There have always been Stratocasters in my life. My father was bitten by the Stratocaster bug when he began listening to the likes of Hendrix, Rory Gallagher and Hank Marvin. I used to stay weekends at my father's house and one day when I was eight we took all his Stratocasters outside to photograph them. I had a ball setting them up on their stands in the garden and writing a description and poorly chosen nickname for each guitar. His collection consisted of his favourite 1961 Stratocaster, which has been used for many years, a 1977 Stratocaster finished in a green Burns sunburst style with rosewood neck and black plastics, a particularly playable 1974 hardtail Stratocaster in natural with a maple neck, and a 1979 tobacco sunburst Stratocaster that was in such perfect condition I was too scared to touch it. His collection would be changing all the time, but I remember a 1954 fortieth anniversary Stratocaster with two cases that I used to show to my guitar-playing friends, which was tricky as it lived in a private section at the top of the house! The other Stratocaster I'll never forget was a 1957 reissue fitted with an original 1950s bridge. It had been aged so well that a fingernail would dent what was left of the finish. This guitar had it all: tone, great weight and the look of a genuine 1950s Stratocaster. My father, in a moment of madness at a guitar show, sold it for £250. I nearly cried.

## 1995 Squier Silver Series Stratocaster, Black, Maple Neck

My memory of this guitar is probably better than the actual instrument. It had all the Stratocaster features, including tremolo and three pickups, and I used it throughout late primary and early high school. I'd been pestering my father for years until at last on 7 November (father's birthday!) he succumbed. He told me to get in the car as we were going to get my first 'Stratocaster'. I spotted it as soon as we walked in the shop since it looked like Jimi Hendrix's guitar from the Isle of Wight film I had seen so many times. I sat with it and fell in love. After some haggling with the shop owner the guitar was mine. It was my main squeeze until I part-exchanged it for Skye two years later.

Looking back, the guitar did not play too well and had a hideously badly shaped body, but since I couldn't play it properly that didn't matter.

## 1996 Fender Mexican Standard Stratocaster, Red, Rosewood Neck

I bought this guitar a week after my thirteenth birthday. I was smitten. I had the neck refinished with a vintage tint and added a trio of Lace Sensor pickups myself. The guitar was the coolest thing I owned. Around this time my fascination for Jimi Hendrix was taking off, however, and soon what I really wanted was a white Stratocaster. This guitar ended up being part-exchanged for Skye.

## 1997 Fender Mexican Standard Stratocaster, White, Rosewood Neck

As expected, I got one, though I had to save for nearly a year to afford it. I now had three Stratocasters which I loved. The guitar seemed faultless to me. It was identical to the red model apart from the modifications I had made. Being only thirteen at the time, I broke the white model's volume pot trying to add a smart tortoiseshell pickguard. I used Blu-Tack to put it back on and sold it – 'Sorry' to the guys at the shop.

## Fender USA Standard Stratocaster, Sonic Blue, Maple Neck

This is Skye. She was my all-time baby. I loved everything about this guitar. Actually, I nearly ended up with a sun-faded yellow Stratocaster instead of Skye, but the shop generously let me have my choice. Either way, I wanted an American Stratocaster and nothing was going to stop me. Skye went through a few pickup changes; I added some AMG pickups that were far cheaper than the EMGs or genuine Fender Lace Sensors I would happily have killed for! The guitar also ended up with one Lace Sensor found during a family holiday in Florida. Then there was a hot rails pickup I bought from a small ad in *Guitarist* magazine, but that went back to stock when I got bored burning myself on my soldering iron. The guitar is presumably now somewhere in the south of England. I have seen identical Stratocasters but never with the N7207847 serial number. It's not a valuable guitar but I bought it new and remember the good times!

## 1979 Fender Stratocaster Hardtail, Black, Maple Neck

I bought this guitar while I still owned Skye and wanted a big headstock model. This black Stratocaster was bought just before vintage mania kicked off and I paid the princely sum of £299. You'd have to put another £1,000 on top of that to get it today. The guitar was short lived. It was heavy, played badly, in poor condition and, above all, would not stay in tune. That £299 seems quite a lot now. This guitar, along with Skye, was foolishly part exchanged for a second-hand SRV Strat.

## Fender Stevie Ray Vaughan Signature Series Stratocaster, Three-Tone Sunburst, Rosewood Neck

The worst thing about this guitar is that to buy it I parted with Skye. It was in Guitar Village in Farnham and I had to part-exchange all my current gear: the 1979 hardtail and Skye, a Fender deluxe 112 amplifier and a Hughes & Kettner Rotosphere pedal that originally cost me nearly £200! I handed over all that for a 1992 Stevie Ray Vaughan Signature model in OK condition but with parts missing, which I then had to work all summer to pay for. And after all that I wasn't happy with my overall purchase.

## Fender 1968 Reissue, Stratocaster Japan, White, Maple Neck

This was my all-time moment of madness. I had become disillusioned with my SRV Stratocaster and, after trying to sell it for five months, I eventually went over to a Sounds Great in Heald Green and handed it over in exchange for one of their excess stock Stratocasters from Japan. The thing looked amazing, played really well and sounded great. I was over the moon with the new Stratocaster. To me the guitar was seriously cool – instant Hendrix, with a big headstock and slim neck – and it rarely went out of tune.

The guitar did not last the year, as I came to realize how smart Stratocasters look with vintage specifications and rosewood necks.

## Fender 1962 Reissue, Stratocaster Japan, Sonic Blue, Rosewood Neck

I took my 1968 Stratocaster to a guitar show to parade round with it and possibly sell it as I was growing bored with it. I loved the guitar but wanted something a little different and rosewood was my first choice. I spotted a 1962 reissue in Sonic Blue sitting behind a vendor's stall. I asked him how much it was up for, but he said it wasn't for sale. I then continued on my way until I was confronted by a dealer who wanted to know what I had and offered £250 cash. I pondered on it and told him I'd come back when I'd decided. I returned to the blue 1962 reissue and enquired again. The vendor explained that he'd just bought the guitar for £200 and loved it. I offered £250 right there and to my amazement he agreed: love is a shallow thing sometimes. I rushed back to sell my white 1968 and did the deal.

## Fender Mexico Classic Series 1960s Stratocaster, White, Rosewood Neck

I kept the 1962 blue Stratocaster for many years until I found out that Fender Mexico Stratocasters like this were getting rave reviews. I was at an age when it really mattered that non-guitarists thought its pale blue was a 'girls' colour' and I was becoming tired of it. By coincidence a friend of mine wanted a guitar, a blue one. I sold him the blue Stratocaster for £300 and put that down as a deposit on the Mexican Classic series Stratocaster. I held my breath until it was in my hands. The guitar was great. I really appreciated the build quality on these early Mexican Classics. I was smitten with my new instrument – it looked like Hendrix's and yet it was all mine.

## Fender Mexico Classic Series 1950s Stratocaster, Surf Green, Maple Neck

A black 1970s Mexican reissue Stratocaster I bought after my birthday was really badly made and was promptly returned. I was now looking for a good backup guitar as I had begun playing live in pubs and bars and wanted something decent in case anything happened to my beloved white Mexican Classic. I found it in another *Guitarist* small ad, a Surf Green 1950s model. The 'flamed neck' and 'Texas Special Pickups' advertised made me want it really badly. The owner in Scotland said he'd send me the guitar before payment to ensure I was happy with it. It turned up a few days later in its gig bag, wrapped in clothes. I lay it on my bed and stared at it. It was probably the best-looking Stratocaster I ever owned. Surf Green is an acquired taste but the finish was nothing compared to the highly flamed maple neck. After sending off the cash in a CD box, I set about making a super Stratocaster out of my two favourites. I went for the ultimate Hendrix Strat and got close. I used the white body, the flamed neck and the rest of the green one's hardware, assembling what was left into a green Strat with a rosewood neck. Still not happy I had a nostalgic moment when watching 'MTV Cribs' …

## Fender Jimi Hendrix Tribute Stratocaster, White, Maple Neck

... I was watching 'MTV Cribs' – I'm not proud of it, but there you go. There was a feature on some rock star's abode and he was telling everyone about his house. When he mentioned his guitars he showed the cameraman an Ace Frehley Gibson Les Paul. He then opened a black Tolex case to reveal a Jimi Hendrix tribute Stratocaster. At once I remembered when they arrived in the shops, failed to sell and then vanished from the Fender catalogue along with any Hendrix links. I used to hang around a shop where there was a brand new Hendrix Stratocaster behind the desk. I would beg the salesmen to let me try it but no one would – not surprising, really, since no twelve-year-old has £849 in his pocket. I knew I'd never get one and so forgot about it. Later, when I had a job and money to my name, my father told me about how a 'new' website called eBay had all kinds of cool guitars. I asked him to keep an eye out for a Hendrix Stratocaster. One popped up in London that had not sold because the seller did not have the right case or any accessories, and for some reason the string tree had been moved slightly to the left. The dilemma was that I had no cash but two good Stratocasters for sale, while the guy needed a buyer quick. I took a trip to the bank and the guitar was mine with the help of a loan. I had one – finally.

## Fender 1962 Reissues (One White, One Refinished Yellow)

I was so obsessed with keeping my Hendrix Stratocaster clean and tidy that it got very little use. A large Christmas present from my grandparents gave me the money to buy whatever Stratocaster I wanted. I went for two reissues: a brand new 1962 reissue in white and a cheap second-hand model refinished in yellow. I had to travel to Derby and my then girlfriend complained all the way. When we arrived the car battery died, so I had no choice but to buy the guitar if I wanted the seller to help me! The yellow didn't last as I sent it off to be refinished in white and then fitted various pickups in it. Weirdly enough, I met Meat Loaf while I owned the refinished Stratocaster and had him sign the rear. Good tale. Shame I don't own the guitar any more. I sold it to the singer of a band I was in: the guitar never played right anyway!

## Fender Custom Shop 1969 NOS Stratocaster, Black, Maple Neck

While working in a guitar shop that dealt heavily in Fender products, I asked Steve, the Fender rep and a good friend, about Custom Shop Stratocasters and in particular the 1969 NOS. This was my all-time favourite Stratocaster, identical to Hendrix's number one. I have loved the black and maple combination all of my life and now the time had come to get a guitar I would never part with. Steve explained that it was the most unpopular Custom Shop time machine Stratocaster made and that I'd never see one in the UK unless it was paid for in advance. Shame. I looked around and found nothing. One day Steve phoned to say he was at a meeting and had been given a list of Stratocasters and Telecasters that had been hanging around the warehouse, occasionally going out in reps' cars but never sold. These guitars were the ugly ducklings and mine was on the list. I asked Steve to show me the guitar as I didn't think it was the real deal. He drove all the way from Halifax to west Sussex and then back up to Chester. By sheer chance I was reading a *Univibes* article on Jimi's black 1968 Stratocaster as Steve walked in with a tatty cardboard box. I opened the case and stared for a few seconds at my dream Stratocaster. I then plugged it into a Marshall JCM800 combo and my mind was made up. The guitar was mine and has since played many gigs, been knocked, burned, signed by Robin Trower at a gig, had a Hendrix decal added to the rear and been re-fretted. It is still much loved.

I have had other Stratocasters, but these are the ones I always remember. I do enjoy other types of guitars, having a soft spot for Flying Vs, for example, as well as the ever desirable 1968 Gibson Les Paul custom, Telecasters from the late 1960s, small-bodied Martin Acoustics, Gibson SG customs ... the list is endless. It just goes to show that there is a story behind every guitar, whether new or second-hand.

## 1968 Stratocaster, White, Maple Neck, Apparently Genuine

I fell hard for this one. I believed it was a genuine 1968 Stratocaster, which is the Holy Grail for any Hendrix fan. I traded a 1976 Fender twin reverb amplifier, the mint 1962 Stratocaster and a cheap Mexican 1950s Stratocaster I had acquired two weeks before (I'd fitted Lace Sensors and hated it). The 1968 Stratocaster looked, felt and sounded right, but something wasn't right. I didn't care because I wanted this guitar so badly. I then did some research and realized to my horror that I'd bought the most expensive Tokai in the world. The guitar was a complete fake. A dealer expressed interest in my Tokai, asked about its origin and claimed the body was a Fender 1968 original. I wasn't so sure but went with the flow. When he offered me half my money back I snapped his hand off and bought my 'number one'.

OPPOSITE: This is my favourite black Stratocaster. I have owned over 180 Stratocasters and have actually thinned down my collection to just owning this one as a gigging guitar. It is a 2003 Fender custom shop 1969 NOS Stratocaster. The guitar has had very minor modifications and is signed by Robin Trower under the pickguard. It also has a Sticker from Guitar Experience in Chester (2005–2009) where the guitar arrived from Fender.

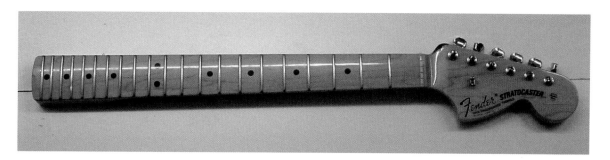

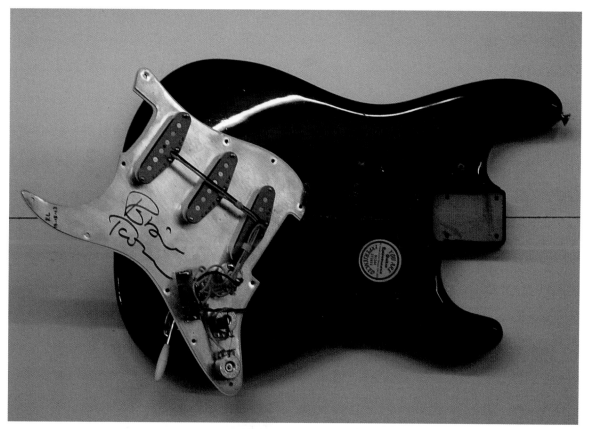

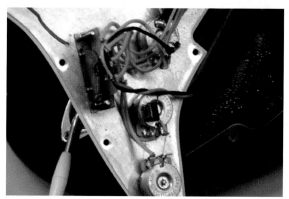

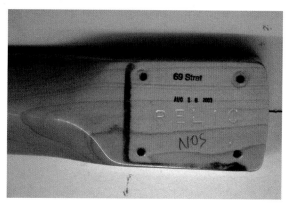

Here is a limited edition John Mayer Stratocaster that I bought in the USA. The finish is a unique Cypress Mica Green, which has never been seen on any other guitar other than this.

Another custom shop 1969 relic I bought to use as a back-up for my black NOS model. This guitar did not feel as good to me as the black model.

# CHAPTER ELEVEN

# STRATOCASTER GALLERY

Here are complete shots of a clean 1963 Stratocaster. It is advised that anyone thinking of buying a vintage Stratocaster should familiarize themselves with certain points that can later be used for reference when buying, to avoid buying a fake. In particular, take note of the electrics, the font used on the neck date and the extra hole hidden behind the 'D' Tuner on the headstock. This particular example was dismantled and photographed by the author and is one of the cleanest 1963 Stratocasters around.

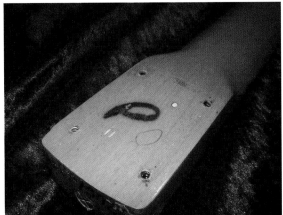

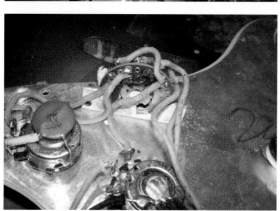

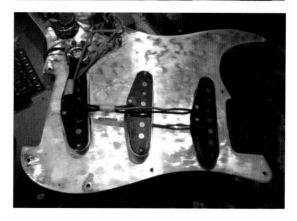

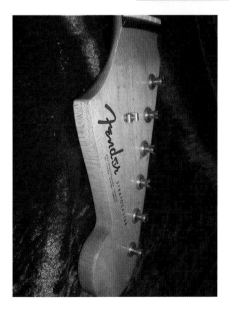

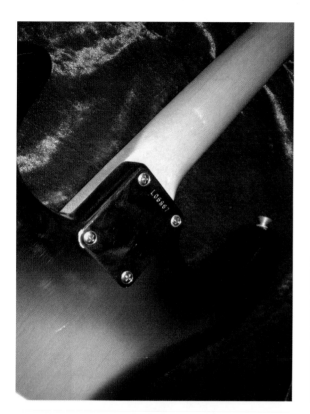

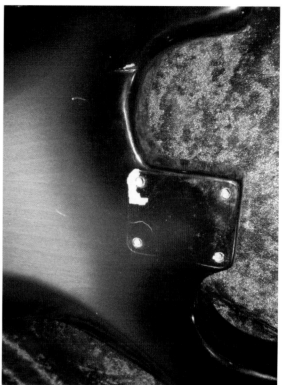

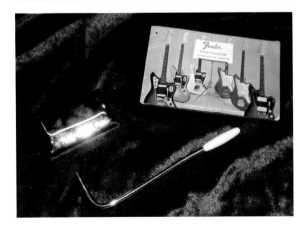

# SIGNATURE STRATOCASTERS

Since their introduction with the Eric Clapton Signature model in 1989, Fender's signature series Stratocasters have gone from strength to strength. The range has grown with a stream of current and long-standing players being honoured by making available to the public designs based on their very own Stratocaster. This may be just a collection of useful or selective improvements made by the players themselves, or it may be an attempt to pass on some of the player's magic.

## Eric Clapton Stratocaster, 1985–

The Eric Clapton Signature series followed the retirement of his famous mongrel of a Stratocaster named 'Blackie', which he had purchased during the early 1970s after the death of Jimi Hendrix. The guitar itself is by no means original. It was one of several vintage Stratocasters that Eric bought for about $100 each. He than assessed each one on its individual merit: some necks were too large, some too small, but one felt right, and so on.

Eric assembled 'Blackie' himself and this quickly became his number one guitar for the following decade. The other Stratocasters were simply reassembled with various parts and given away to friends such as George Harrison and Pete Townshend. 'Blackie' was retired when the guitar was no longer fit for use – it was simply worn out.

In 1985 Eric Clapton approached Fender to make a replica model for him with the exact specifications of 'Blackie', but with slightly upgraded electrics and pickups. The collaboration was the first in a long line of Stratocasters known as the signature series. The Eric Clapton model has been the most successful of all the signature models and remains in production. The first time Fender met with Eric to discuss the Eric Clapton model, they supplied him with the last of the factory-run Elite Stratocasters and some USA Vintage reissue '57 Stratocasters. The first run of the Eric Clapton Stratocaster was to be a nice combination of the two.

### 1ST RUN ERIC CLAPTON SIGNATURE STRATOCASTERS

The 1st run Eric Clapton Stratocaster was to feature a selected alder body modelled heavily on an early 1950s Stratocaster. The neck was designed on a 1950s profile but incorporating the unusual 'V' shape, which was very noticeable on 'Blackie'. The guitar incorporated a set of Gold Lace Sensor pickups and the TBX unit was fitted with a mid-range boost powered by a 9-volt battery. The headstock featured the classic spaghetti logo as well as Clapton's signature on the tip. Models in the classic black finish read 'Blackie' underneath Eric's signature. The guitar was sold with a blocked off tremolo unit, which meant that they came with a tremolo fitted but a block of wood was inserted between the tremolo block and the body to seize the tremolo, but still give good resonance due to the springs. The guitars were fitted with Bi-Flex truss rods and a micro-tilt was installed. The Eric Clapton Stratocaster 1st run was available in black, Pewter, Torino Red, Olympic White and Candy Apple Green (this was due to Eric's love of the green used by 7UP on their drinks cans). The guitars were sold in a classic tweed case and retailed at around $1,300.

### 2ND RUN ERIC CLAPTON STRATOCASTER

The Eric Clapton Stratocaster went through a few changes in early 2003. The pickups were changed from Gold Lace Sensors to Fender's brand new 'Noiseless' single coils, which were designed to give a Lace Sensor-style sound that would accentuate the player's style and give more of a single-coil tone. The newer model has been an even greater success. The Eric Clapton Signature model is one of the most popular instruments for session musicians worldwide.

### ERIC CLAPTON CUSTOM SHOP COLLABORATIONS

Eric Clapton has been a major influence on guitar players over the last two decades and it is no surprise that Fender has honoured him with a few Custom Shop models. There is, for example, a Custom Shop version of his signature Stratocaster that is apparently identical to the one Eric takes on tour. A limited edition of fifty of these have been finished by New York graffiti artist John 'CRASH' Matos. There is also a Stratocaster in the same dark blue as Eric's Mercedes-Benz. The 'Gold' Stratocaster is a work of art finished in 22 carat gold leaf. For the Masterbuilt Tribute series, Fender directly cloned the original 'Blackie' Stratocaster with all its wear and tear. Fender promised this would be an exact replica of the original, although at around £10,000 it's a lot to pay for a guitar that is technically 'worn out'.

## Yngwie Malmsteen Stratocaster, 1987–

Swedish 'shredder' Yngwie Malmsteen was honoured by Fender in 1987 for his contribution to modern music with his own brand of neo-classical heavy metal. Fender teamed up to create a Stratocaster bearing his name to be added alongside the Eric Clapton model in the signature series. The guitar is loosely based upon a 1956 Stratocaster Yngwie then owned. He was one of the few guitar players still using unmodified Stratocasters in their original form and Marshall amplifiers, just as Jimi Hendrix had done. The Malmsteen signature model was the first in the Stratocaster signature series to feature a scalloped fretboard. This was an idea that came to Yngwie when a lute was brought in to a guitar repair shop in Sweden where he was working. Yngwie scalloped a few of his Stratocasters and this was to be a standard feature on the signature model. The pickups were made by DiMarzio. The models Yngwie favoured were HBS-3. These are stacked humbuckers, in order to give a thicker humbucker-like tone, but will fit in a single coil-sized rout depending on body depth. These were fitted in the neck and bridge positions, and in the middle position was the flush pole piece American Standard.

The bridge and hardware were a cross between 1950s and 1990s: the tuners were Kluson-styled and the bridge was the 'powdered steel' type featured on the American Standard Stratocaster. A TBX tone control was wired to the neck and bridge. The Yngwie Malmsteen Stratocaster was also available as a Japanese model made with similar electrics but modelled on an early 1970s Stratocaster with the large headstock. These guitars are rarely seen. Yngwie altered the cosmetics of his signature model by adding a Bi-Flex truss rod and a 1968–69 era headstock incorporating a logo of the period. Many feel this is due to Yngwie's love of Jimi Hendrix, and in particular the '68 maple-necked Stratocaster he used at the Woodstock Festival in 1969. The Yngwie Malmsteen Signature series has been available in both Sonic Blue and cream, Yngwie's favourite Stratocaster colour. The guitars were sold in a tweed case and originally retailed at around $1,200.

## Robert Cray Stratocaster, 1990–

The Robert Cray Signature model Stratocaster, released in 1990, is based on Cray's two favourite model Stratocasters: a 1958 hardtail (non-tremolo) Stratocaster, which he has always preferred for its crisp and punchier sound, and a 1964 Inca Silver Stratocaster. Together these two guitars have created his unique blend of clean blues. Cray has been a major player in guitar circles for many years due to his ice-cold, stinging style of playing. The signature model features a lightweight alder body, based on his favourite 1958 model, along with a 1964-style, oval, rosewood-capped fretboard. The neck is fairly chunky to mimic Cray's original model. The guitar has vintage fretwire, which is slightly thinner than its jumbo counterparts. The model features relatively standard electrics: a trio of specially designed pickups, a five-way switch and the usual volume and two tones. The guitar also came complete with the vintage bridge unit, styled similarly to that of a Telecaster, with six ferrules on the back of the body for through-body stringing. This style of Fender manufacture has been shown to increase sustain and keep tuning more stable than on models equipped with a tremolo. This was the first signature model available without a tremolo setup at the bridge, eighteen years before that for Billy Corgan of the Smashing Pumpkins (see below). The Robert Cray Stratocaster was available in Inca Silver, similar to his original, and Violet. The Robert Cray Signature model was not intended for public release but only to custom order.

In the early 2000s Fender USA custom orders were moved to the Custom Shop line of artist models, which have only limited availability as there are very few places where they are advertised. Late in 2005, however, Fender released the Robert Cray model for general sale. This time, while remaining a custom order model, it was based on a Mexican-built Stratocaster, which fits neatly with the Classic series although is not advertised as such. The build quality and playability is very similar to the Classic models from Mexico. The Mexican Robert Cray has the same basic features as its USA brother, but polyurethane paint is used on the neck and body, and the pickups are Mexican-designed and built. The model has a padded gig bag, which is suitable for purpose.

## Jeff Beck Stratocaster, 1990–

In 1987 Fender asked Jeff Beck if he would be interested in becoming another signature on the famous Stratocaster headstock. His witty reply that he didn't deserve it was the probable reason why the Beck Stratocaster took another three years to arrive in the shops. The model was loosely based on the Stratocaster Plus model that Beck had been using in recent years. The 1st run model Beck turned out to be possibly the best value, but also the most unlikely model, that Fender had ever made.

### 1ST RUN JEFF BECK STRATOCASTER

These guitars were not big sellers and are usually found in the back of guitar shops collecting dust waiting for a player with big enough hands to buy it. The guitar's initial run featured an alder body and a maple neck with Pau Ferro fretboard. This is a distinctive type of rosewood, cultivated in Brazil, that is usually slightly lighter in colour and is used in furniture manufacturing and for guitar and basses. It is used due to the scarcity of Brazilian rosewood, which otherwise is most desirable owing to its similarity to ebony. There were Gold Lace Sensor pickups in the neck and middle position, and a 'dually' Lace Sensor humbucker in the bridge position with a button next to the tone controls to activate the full capacity of the dually bridge pickup. The guitar used the two-point tremolo system from the American Standard or Plus models.

After its release, Fender's biggest problem was with the neck. If you imagine Jeff Beck asking for the biggest possible neck on his signature Stratocaster, and Fender basically supplying him with a baseball bat, you'd have the right idea. The neck was indescribable. It was too big for many customers but there were enough die-hard Beck fans out there to warrant a market. The neck was fretted with twenty-two medium Jumbo frets for big string bends. The machine heads on the 1st run were locking Sperzel models, while the LSR roller nut fitted is a superb tool as it has very little friction between string and nut itself and keeps tuning very stable. All this was packaged inside a tweed case and sold at around £1,200 when new; it was available in Midnight Purple, Surf Green and Olympic White. The guitar is now extinct as Fender decided to revamp the model for its second run. The first Jeff Beck Stratocaster can be seen in the 1991 compilation of Jeff's work, *Beckology*. Fender allowed Sony to use the signature Stratocaster's tweed case for the design of the box itself, while the booklet inside has a good shot of the signature Stratocaster in midnight purple in its fur-lined tweed case.

### 2ND RUN JEFF BECK STRATOCASTER

The 2nd run Jeff Beck Stratocaster was welcomed by guitarists in 2003 as it now offered a thinner neck, three single-coil, hot, noiseless pickups and a carved neck heel, which were all well-received adjustments. The 2nd run is much more player friendly. It is offered both in the USA signature range and as a custom artist model. The latter has all the same features but, basically being constructed with slightly better components, is exactly what Jeff uses when touring. This model is usually found in Olympic White or Surf Green.

# Stevie Ray Vaughan Stratocaster, 1992–

A firm favourite in the signature series of Stratocasters, this was originally commissioned before SRV's untimely death on 27 August 1990 when, having recently beaten drink and drug addiction, and immediately after a concert with Eric Clapton and Robert Cray, his helicopter crashed into a mountainside in Alpine Valley, near East Troy, Wisconsin. In numerous polls since then SRV has been voted since one of the best blues guitarists. He famously used a beaten up Stratocaster assembled from a 1959 body and an early 1960s neck. This was modified with gold-plated hardware and an oddball left-handed tremolo system as a nod to his hero Jimi Hendrix. The guitar was fitted with high output pickups that, coupled with his gauge 13 strings and a high action that most found unplayable, resulted in Stevie Ray Vaughan's unique and never bettered tone. The Stevie Ray Vaughan Stratocaster is a desirable model owing to its three-tone sunburst alder body and Pau Ferro fretboard, along with the introduction of Texas Special pickups. The guitar also featured a unique pickguard as a tribute to SRV. On his original model he had added reflective 'SRV' let-

tering on the black pickguard. On the first couple of signature models this was printed on in white, but when Fender realized that the pickguards were prone to scratching, the next step was to engrave the lettering into the plastic so it would stay forever.

The SRV Stratocaster is basically a hot rodded '62 reissue with a slightly larger neck at 12in (30.5cm) radius, hotter pickups and Dunlop 6105 frets, which are larger than the standard issue. The tuners are gold-plated Kluson styles and the bridge is a vintage model, albeit left-handed.

No other changes have been made apart from usually unnoticeable contours and body shapes.

Two other models connected with SRV have been made since the introduction of the signature models. The first is a direct replica of his original 'number one' mongrel, which had all the cigarette burns and showed exactly the same wear and tear SRV had given his own model. These were strictly limited to 100 units worldwide and retailed at about £10,000. This guitar has become a hot commodity in collectors' circles. The second SRV-related guitar came about when Guitar Centre (USA) bought Stevie's original 'Lenny' Stratocaster for around $650,000 at an Eric Clapton Crossroads auction at Christie's. The guitar was also a mongrel, this time with a 1950s neck and a 1965 three-tone sunburst body, which was given to Stevie by his wife Lenora. He composed the ever beautiful 'Lenny' on this guitar, which had been stripped of its original finish and varnished. The front of the body featured an inlay that looked like something off a highly priced coffee table. On the back was the autograph of the baseball legend Mickey Mantle, which was written in permanent marker after SRV met Mantle at a baseball game where he'd been asked to play the national anthem. The bridge was a retrofit model that suited tremolo use. The Fender Tribute Lenny came exactly as the original: Anvil flight case, worn neck and body, and a replica Mickey Mantle autograph on the back. The package included a replica 'notes' strap as well as certificates, backstage passes and DVDs of SRV playing 'Lenny'. This guitar, which was limited to 250 units worldwide and retails for around £13,000, has not been as popular as the first tribute model.

## Richie Sambora Stratocaster, 1993–97

Bon Jovi guitar player Richie Sambora was honoured with a signature Stratocaster in early 1993. It was withdrawn when demand ceased in 1997. This guitar was the archetypal 1990s rock Stratocaster, featuring a Floyd Rose tremolo system and a humbucker in the bridge position.

The Stratocaster was finished in Candy Apple Red, white or Cherry Sunburst, similar to that of a Gibson, and featured a 1950s style alder body with a maple neck that was built to a 12in radius for more of a Gibson feel. Sambora opted for a DiMarzio Pro PAF humbucker in the bridge and two Texas Special pickups for the neck and middle. The Floyd Rose was double locking, which meant that the nut also has a locking system that clamps the string down for optimum stability or headaches, depending on which you prefer. The electrics also incorporated the TBX tone circuit.

The Richie Sambora model was generally marketed by Fender for offshore manufacture, mainly in Japan.

## Dick Dale Stratocaster, 1992–

The Dick Dale Stratocaster has always been a custom order Stratocaster due to the limited market. Perceived by many Stratocaster fans as the ugly duckling in the signature series, the Dick Dale Stratocaster is finished in gold sparkle paint and features a reverse headstock, since Dick Dale is left-handed. The model features an alder body, three custom-wound 1950s pickups, a toggle switch for the neck and middle positions for out-of-phase sounds, reverse angle bridge pickup, no tone controls, twenty-one vintage frets and a gold Chartreuse Sparkle finish. The guitar is designed and built for Dick himself and appeals to very few.

## Alex Gregory Stratocaster

The Alex Gregory Signature model never actually made it into the Fender catalogue but was an unusual seven-string Stratocaster. The guitar featured three Black Lace Sensor pickups, a two-point tremolo system and twenty-four frets, which together allowed the player to float into classical music with the use of effects. It had been given the name 'Guitolin' by Gregory. The guitar was a Custom Shop build and there are only two prototypes in existence: one has a reverse headstock and the other is normal.

## Hank Marvin Stratocaster, 1990–92

The Hank Marvin Stratocaster was commissioned by Fender's UK distributor Arbiter in the early 1990s. The guitar was basically the same as the original 1958 model that Hank had custom ordered many years before (*see* Chapter 4). The guitar was limited to twenty-five units and had a high retail price. The guitar had three Gold Lace Sensor pickups wired into an active circuit, as well as the two-point tremolo in gold and a Graphtech nut. These guitars also feature Hank's own 'Ezy-mute' tremolo, which allows the player to mute strings while holding the arm itself.

The other Hank Marvin Signature models are all manufactured in Japan, the first being a Squier model based on a 1950s Stratocaster similar to that copied for an early JV Squier, with similar playability. The model has no extra features apart from the Fiesta Red finish and Hank's signature on the headstock. The second was a Japanese Fender reissue known as the Hank Marvin Signature model. This was another 1950s reissue, similar to the Japanese 'collectable' series, though with Hank's signature on the headstock. The Hank Marvin Signature models in all countries of manufacture never made it to the Fender USA catalogues, since Hank and the Shadows are not as well known as they are in the UK.

## Bonnie Raitt Stratocaster, 1992–97

Little is documented about Bonnie Raitt's Signature model Stratocaster. During my early high school years, just as my Stratocaster fascination was beginning to take hold, I used to stare at Bonnie's signature Stratocaster through a shop window in Chester and dream of one day owning one. Owing to its rarity I have yet to achieve this. The model itself is now discontinued, but has a great look and specification.

Bonnie specified that her model be based on her own original late 1960s Stratocaster, which has the nickname 'Old Brown'. The signature model featured a lightweight alder body, Pau Ferro rosewood neck and a late 1960s large headstock and four-bolt neck setup. Bonnie insisted that she wanted no royalties for her model, but they should be paid to a charity fund that encouraged children to explore music and have decent instruments. The eye-catching guitars featured a deep blue sunburst never seen on a pro-duction-run Stratocaster before; three-tone sunburst was also an option. A pearloid pickguard housed the standard Stratocaster layout of volume and two tones, controlling three Texas Special pickups. There was a spaghetti logo on the peghead, which is unusual for the large headstock. Bonnie opted for the Bi-Flex truss rod system on the headstock. The machine heads were Kluson replicas and the model was fitted with a vintage-style tremolo. The choice of gold-plated hardware led some to speculate that Bonnie had been influenced by the guitar of her close friend, Stevie Ray Vaughan. The guitar was released in a limited run of 200 guitars, featuring birds-eye maple on the back of the neck and headstock. These 200 models were all hand signed on the pickguard by Bonnie. The guitars also came complete with a tweed case. These models are mow incredibly rare and many belong to Bonnie Raitt fans around the world.

## Ritchie Blackmore Stratocaster, 1990–

Ritchie Blackmore's use of Stratocasters throughout his time in Deep Purple and Rainbow made him an obvious choice for a signature model. This guitar ended up going through three different runs and is now only available through the Fender Custom Shop at high cost. His first signature model came from the USA and featured an ash body, two Seymour Duncan 'quarter pound' pickups (one in the neck position and one in the bridge), and a specific absence of middle position pickup, since Blackmore has claimed that the middle pickup gets in the way of his technique. This is seen in footage of Blackmore playing his old 1970s models and lowering the middle pickup completely below the pickguard. This method was also preferred by Robbie Robertson of The Band. The Blackmore Sig-nature model also sported a scalloped fingerboard like the Yngwie Malmsteen Signature Stratocaster years before. Just as there is a debate as to who came up with the scalloped neck on a Stratocaster, so there are many who despise the scalloped board. The gui-tar featured a rosewood neck, large headstock and vintage hardware in accordance with the 1970s char-acteristics.

The 2nd run of the Blackmore Stratocaster was manufactured by Fender in Japan as a limited edition in 1997. It was similar to the first run but had a dum-my pickup in the middle position to help improve the interference problems usually associated with Stra-tocasters. These guitars feature a basswood body as well as the scalloped twenty-one fret neck. Unusually for a signature model, Ritchie Blackmore's signature doesn't feature anywhere on the guitar. The pickups were identical to those featured on the first run.

The 3rd run of Blackmore's signature model was made in the Fender Custom Shop and was an all-new, updated version of the previous runs. It came com-plete with a Roland GK-2 Synthesizer pickup, which allows the player to create many artificial synthesizer effects such as orchestral violins. The pickups were also changed to Gold Lace Sensor models, which

Blackmore preferred, before later switching to AGI models. The bridge was also switched to a two-point tremolo system. The guitar also underwent a major change in construction; it was one of the first models to have a set neck, similar to that of a Gibson, as well as twenty-two frets. This guitar is now only available as a custom order.

## John Mayer Stratocaster, 2005–

The Grammy winning Stratocaster fanatic John Mayer is one of the newest additions to the signature family. At a time when many believe the design of the Stratocaster has been pushed as far as it will go, Mayer has added a different approach to his model. Mayer saved up for a 1996 Stevie Ray Vaughan Signature model after he left high school and he still uses it on stage today. His signature model reflects the Stevie Ray Vaughan influence. The Stratocaster itself features an alder body, Indian rosewood neck and vintage hardware. The guitar's pickups, known as 'Big Dippers', are specially designed by John for more mid-range. The guitar has a comfortable 9.5in (24.1cm) neck radius. Having used an SRV Stratocaster for many years, John opted for Dunlop 6105 frets on his model. The interesting thing about the Mayer signature model is that the string tree is placed farther away from the nut, similar to that on an early 1950s Telecaster, in order to allow the player to create bends behind the nut more easily. Another Fender first was the removal of the tremolo's cover plate, a modification made by many players, including two of Mayer's biggest influences, Jimi Hendrix and Stevie Ray Vaughan. The guitar is wired differently to allow a tone control on the bridge pickup as well as the middle and neck. Players often wonder why Fender haven't done this on every Stratocaster since 1954, since it requires only about an extra 5in (12.7cm). The guitar is the only signature model made in collaboration with a company known as Incase, who are good friends with John and manufacture cutting-edge cases for iPods, laptops and various other items. The case is a very good cross between a gig bag and a hard case.

The John Mayer Stratocaster was originally sold in three-colour sunburst with a red tortoiseshell pickguard or in Shoreline Gold with a burgundy 'competition stripe' down the right-hand side of the body front. Since the first models were released, Shoreline Gold has been replaced by Olympic White with mint-green and cream plastics. There was also a limited run of 100 made in Charcoal Frost metallic, offset by a grey competition stripe. These guitars are reportedly John's favourite. They are also very scarce and command high prices second-hand. The other limited model was finished in a colour known as Cypress Mica, a faded army green finish that looks almost grey up close, and came complete with an Incase bag in a different colourway from the first ones. Limited models from John Mayer feature cream Tonemaster amplifier knobs, which differentiate them from standard run models.

## Hellecasters Signature models, 1997–98

Jerry Donahue, Will Ray (Telecaster signature model) and John Jorgenson could easily be described as the greatest session guitarists on the planet, so it seems only fitting that Fender should honour them with a set of signature guitars named after their band The Hellecasters.

Since Jerry Donahue is famous for using a Telecaster and having named a solo album *Telecasting*, it seemed slightly odd that Jerry should have a signature Stratocaster (he has since been honoured with a signature Telecaster). The Jerry Donahue Stratocaster is as rare as the sight of Jerry holding it. It was manufactured in Japan and was based on a 1950s Stratocaster. It features a deep blue, slightly sunburst finish on the body and a black pickguard with white pickups and knobs. The guitar is an oddball intended to complete a set with the other two instruments. The only important feature to set it apart from other guitars was a metal plate added under the bridge pickup to emulate a more Telecaster tone. Aside from this, the guitar has

'Hellecasters' inlaid at the twelfth fret, the sole feature shared by all three in the set. This guitar also has the odd John Mayer-style string tree placement, a Bi-Flex truss rod and Jerry's signature on the headstock tip.

The John Jorgenson model was a completely different animal, sporting enough sparkle to blind most people. The body was lightweight alder finished in Black Sparkle paint. The gold sparkle pickguard housed three high-output Seymour Duncan split pickups. Their odd appearance makes these pickups look similar to those used on twelve-string Fenders from the mid- to late 1960s. The hardware was gold plated and incorporated the two-point tremolo and domed Telecaster knobs. The neck had gold sparkle inlays as well as the mandatory 'Hellecaster' logo at the twelfth fret. For a bit of a Jimi Hendrix influence, Jorgenson requested a reversed late 1960s headstock. A Bi-Flex truss rod was fitted, as were Schaller sealed tuners. The headstock logo was a transition-style Fender with 'HELLECASTER' next to it, followed by John's signature on the headstock tip.

## Mark Knopfler Stratocaster, 2004–

When it was released the Mark Knopfler Signature model caused some controversy in the guitar-related media as many players thought that it offered nothing new and just had Knopfler's signature on the headstock. There were a few things going on under the paint, however, that had players spending. The Dire Straits guitar player had been a big fan of Hank Marvin and Stratocasters from an early age. When Fender approached him he decided to model his signature model on an early 1960s Stratocaster he had refinished in Fiesta Red. This model is an incredibly lightweight guitar since Knopfler decided to have the ash body drained of all its moisture to achieve the correct weight. This results in a hollow resonant tone favoured by many. The guitar was directly based on a 1960s Stratocaster and retains the identical layout. The pickups chosen are the Texas Special models fa-

voured by Knopfler. The finish is a new colour known as Hot Rod Red, which looks somewhere between Dakota Red and Fiesta Red, and it is housed in a brown Tolex case. The guitar is now a much loved entry in the Fender catalogue.

## Eric Johnson Stratocaster, 2005–

Eric Johnson is known as the 'Texas Tone Hound', a tag that has transferred to his signature model Stratocaster, which is available in two-tone sunburst, Candy Apple Red, White Blonde and black. (A three-tone sunburst model is available only to customers of Wildwood Guitars in Colorado, who commissioned a limited run for themselves.) The guitar features an extremely lightweight two-piece alder body as well as a nicely figured maple neck. It is the most expensive signature model guitar not manufactured in the Custom Shop. The guitar has interesting modifications that contribute to the overall tone. There is no paint where the tremolo block is fitted to the body, since Johnson believes that this is the main point of resonance. This is also why the rear tremolo cover has been removed.

The neck is a V-shape smoothed into a gentle U-shape further up the neck. The frets are medium jumbo-sized and the headstock is cut slightly deeper, thus avoiding the use of string trees. The machine heads are Kluson-Gotoh replicas and also staggered to alleviate this. There is no Johnson signature, but the guitar does have an engraved neck plate with a 'Tiki' style engraving of a guitar player with the initials 'E' and 'J'. The electrics are similar to that of the Mayer, allowing tone control for all pickups. The pickups are of no specific name but were closely designed by Johnson and Fender. He reportedly sent back around fifteen sets until he was satisfied: rumour has it that Johnson can tell the difference in the brand of batteries used in his Fuzz Face pedals. His signature guitar also has slightly more of a cutaway on the lower body horn for better upper fret access, a welcome feature that does not interfere with the original Stratocaster shape. This guitar is readily available and highly play-able with great tones to match. It is housed in a mid-1960s blonde Tolex case with plush black interior.

## George Harrison Stratocaster, 2001

While not technically a signature model, this has been linked to Harrison owing to the Beatles connection during the *Rubber Soul* recordings. The guitar itself was a basic 1962 Reissue Stratocaster finished in Sonic Blue, as Harrison's original had been until he attacked it with day-glo paint during the recording and filming of *The Magical Mystery Tour* (1967), when it became 'Rocky'. The guitars were a limited run from 2001 and came complete with a book about Beatles equipment.

## Buddy Guy Stratocaster, 1994–

One of the greatest blues guitar players of all time, Buddy Guy has been a Stratocaster player for many years. Following an endorsement in the early 1980s he used Guild guitars, but switched back shortly after. The model Buddy created with Fender in 1994 was available in sunburst and blonde. The guitar features Lace Sensors and a 25dB mid-boost similar to the Eric Clapton model. Based on some of Buddy's favourite 1950s Stratocasters, the guitar features a strong V-neck shape, a vintage bridge assembly and a Bi-Flex truss rod. The machine heads are Kluson-Gotoh units. This model is manufactured in the USA and comes complete with a tweed case.

There is also a Polka Dot model, which is a celebra-tion of Buddy's career. From an early age he told his mother that he'd eventually have a polka-dot limo and that he'd take her out in it for dinner. Sadly she did not live long enough to see Buddy's rise to stardom, so as a tribute to her Buddy asked Fender to make a

black and white polka-dot finish for his Stratocaster. The guitars featuring this are manufactured in Mexico and are sold without the tweed case, Lace Sensor or active boosts. They are mainly favoured by Buddy Guy fans or players looking for something different. Buddy is occasionally seen with a red and white polka-dot Stratocaster, as opposed to the black and white model available from Fender.

## Rory Gallagher Stratocaster, 2006–

This is not actually part of the signature series, but belongs to the Artist range from the Custom Shop. Rory Gallagher was a true guitar player down to the bone. The man who could sometimes play four sets a night relied on a 1961 Stratocaster bought on hire purchase for about £100 from Crowley's Music on MacCurtain Street in Cork. This was reportedly the first Stratocaster in Ireland and was used heavily un-til Rory's premature death in 1995. The guitar was a three-tone sunburst model that was in poor shape by the time Fender came to create the signature mod-el. Due to Rory's playing style and apparently overly acidic sweat, the paint had pretty much fallen off and left bare wood, albeit with more bumps and chips in the wood than any other famous Stratocaster (except perhaps for SRV's 'number one'). My father, who in-cidentally is from Bangor, near Belfast in Northern Ireland, is a big Rory Gallagher fan and once had gui-tar lessons from Rory himself. According to him the famous Stratocaster was in poor shape even back in the late 1960s and early 1970s, the legacy of acidic sweat and heavy gigging.

It should be noted that the Fender signature model was not actually signed or commissioned by Rory, but was approved by his close brother Donal. The guitar was introduced as more of a tribute than a signature model and only 100 units were intended, but due to heavy demand the guitar was put into production at the Custom Shop with each one being 'replicated' with Rory's wear and tear. The guitars are recreations of all of Rory's modifications over the years of ownership. The tuners are five Sperzel models with one Gotoh on the low 'E' string. The wiring is one master volume and one master tone with a five-way switch. The Fender replica models are not entirely accurate to the original but do feature similar characteristics. The guitar comes complete with a brown Tolex case.

## Tom DeLonge Stratocaster, 2005–6

An interesting model to come off the Mexico production line is the Tom DeLonge Stratocaster, which is the most basic Stratocaster ever made. It was discontinued following the break-up of DeLonge's teenybopper punk band Blink-182. The guitar features a Surf Green, Sonic Blue, black or yellow alder body, pearloid pickguard and a single Seymour Duncan Invader pickup (the company's highest output pickup), along with one single master volume control. The guitar initially had a two-point tremolo, which was replaced by a hardtail unit following production. The guitar had Sperzel locking tuners and a large headstock with the period-correct logo. The guitar features the name 'Tom DeLonge' on an engraved four-bolt neck plate.

The guitar has also been copied by Squier for budget release.

## Jimmie Vaughan Stratocaster, 1997–

The Jimmie Vaughan Stratocaster is a curio produced by the Mexican factory. Jimmie Vaughan is the elder brother of Stevie Ray Vaughan and was playing in and around Texas while Stevie was still a child. The Fender model that bears his name is loosely based on a 1950s Stratocaster. It was originally advertised under the name 'Tex-Mex', owing to its Mexican manufacture and Texan endorsee. This guitar was not actually made as a signature model until Jimmie decided that it should be his main guitar and the Jimmie Vaughan

Tex Mex was born. The guitar is available in white, black and sunburst and is a semi-budget instrument with all the features to make it a professional working guitar. In any Jimmie Vaughan footage the chances are he is using this guitar. Its 1950s styling gives it a single ply pickguard and an alder body, as well as a single-piece maple neck with a small headstock and spaghetti logo. The truss rod adjuster is situated at the top of the neck, similar to a Bi-Flex. The guitar has hotter wound pickups of a similar design to his younger brother's Texas Special models.

## Billy Corgan Stratocaster, 2008–

Smashing Pumpkins guitar player and vocalist Billy Corgan has been using 1970s era Stratocasters for many years. In 2008 Fender honoured him with his own signature model, which is roughly based on a Highway One series Stratocaster, using satin-finished bodies and necks as well as the retro large headstocks. The guitar is available in either black or white. It incorporates a DiMarzio single-coil stacked-rail humbucker, known as the Chopper, in the middle as well as Corgan-designed models in the neck and bridge positions to supply his infamous buzz saw tone. The model features a hardtail bridge and Schaller tuners similar to the Highway One series, as well as two string trees and a Bi-Flex truss rod. The guitar's finishes are monochrome, either black with white pickguard or white with black pickguard. Both options feature a 9.5in (24.1cm) radius maple neck with twenty-two medium jumbo frets. The switching, which incorporates a five-way switch, is an interesting part of the Corgan model:

| | |
|---|---|
| Position 1 | Full humbucking bridge pickup |
| Position 2 | Inside coil of bridge pickup and full humbucking middle pickup |
| Position 3 | Full humbucking middle pickup |
| Position 4 | Full humbucking middle pickup and outside coil of neck pickup |
| Position 5 | Full humbucking neck pickup |

The Corgan Stratocaster is housed in a tweed case and also has the Corgan signature on the back of the headstock. The Billy Corgan Signature Stratocaster is the cheapest of all the American Signature series due to the Highway One influence of its finishing.

## Robin Trower Stratocaster, 2006–

Robin Trower played with Procol Harum from 1967 to 1972, when he left to make his own way as a solo performer. His Robin Trower Band featured bass player James Dewar and various drummers at different periods. Trower has been linked to Jimi Hendrix due his use of a Stratocaster, Marshall Plexi amplifiers, Fuzz Faces and Univibe pedals. Since he had used a Stratocaster for such classic albums as *For Earth Below* and *Bridge of Sighs*, Fender approached Robin for a signature model and set about creating a Custom Shop Artist model as well as a limited run of 100 guitars. The limited run was relatively similar to the production model, apart from including a limited edition Fulltone Deja Vibe pedal (the Univibe replica that Robin currently uses). The guitar was master built by Todd Krause and paraphernalia associated with Robin and the Custom Shop was enclosed, including a certificate and a DVD with interviews and construction footage. The production-run guitar, which has a four-bolt neck and the 'bullet' truss rod, was modelled on the typical 1970s Stratocaster with which Robin is so well associated. It is manufactured with an alder body, in either Olympic White or a deep wine sunburst, and has a maple neck with pearloid dot markers. The guitar also features Sperzel Trim-Lok machine heads, which lock the string as they trim off any excess string ends. The guitar's electrics are set out with the standard one volume and two tones, with two custom designed 1950s pickups in the neck and middle and an unusual Tex-Mex pickup in the bridge position. The parchment-coloured plastics are nicely offset against either the wine or white finish. The Robin Trower Signature model shows Robin's signature on the reverse of the headstock and is housed in a period-correct black Tolex case.

## David Gilmour Stratocaster, 2008–

David Gilmour is well known as one of the most tasteful guitar players in the world. His stellar guitar work on such Pink Floyd albums as *Meddle*, *The Wall* and *Dark Side of the Moon* have earned him the respect of millions of fans worldwide. David has been a fan of Fenders since the early 1960s and his parents gave him a brand new white Telecaster for his twenty-first birthday in 1967. He claims to have always admired players who used Fenders and this explains his choice of a Stratocaster on the main body of Pink Floyd's work.

Since Gilmour has used Fenders for a long time, it seems odd that he was not honoured with a signature model until late 2008, although he apparently declined Fender's initial offer of a signature Stratocaster around the time that Jeff Beck's model was introduced.

Interestingly enough, this followed the publication of *The Black Strat* by Phil Taylor, Gilmour's long-serving guitar technician. This has page after page of detailed insights about Gilmour and his famous guitar. This particular Stratocaster is a firm favourite of Gilmour, a complete hybrid in the manner of Eric Clapton's 'Blackie'. The guitar consists of a heavily modified 1969 black Stratocaster body that has been fitted with XLR inputs, humbuckers, Kahler tremolos and various necks. The guitar appears in its 'clean' original state in the concert film *Live from Pompeii*, where Gilmour sits semi-naked in the sand with his black Strat on his lap, while playing a bit of slide guitar and adding interstellar effects with a wah wah pedal wired backwards and a Fuzz Face pedal. It is, as it sounds, interesting.

The David Gilmour Signature model came as no surprise as Gilmour has played nothing else since he hung up his two Candy Apple Red 1957 reissues with active EMG electronics following the Division Bell tour. These guitars were thought to be his favourites, as he had used them since they were bought new in 1987, but they are no longer in use. David set about reconstructing the black Strat after its stay in the Hard Rock Café chain from 1986 to 1997.

Fender decided that the David Gilmour Stratocaster should be available in two varieties. Purists can buy a Gilmour Stratocaster in the Relic finish, which is slightly distressed in the manner of Gilmour's original. For others there is an NOS model finished in a mint condition.

Both the Relic and the NOS guitars were created to be part of the Custom Shop Artist models series. Rumours abound that these are limited edition models, but that is not the case, although the first 500 guitars sold, in either finish, come with a copy of Phil Taylor's book *The Black Strat*, autographed by the author.

The guitars' specification features one strange addition: in either finish the guitar is finished in black over three-tone sunburst. It is interesting to note that the original Stratocaster is straight black, and that this feature was added later in the design stage. The body wood used is alder, which reflects the original guitar nicely. The one-piece neck is straight grain maple and modelled on an early 1950s Stratocaster with a subtle V shape; this is something Gilmour himself will have specified.

An acquired taste on the Gilmour Stratocaster is the inclusion of the black pickguard, first added to the original model in September 1974. It is offset with white pickup covers, knobs and switch tip, and most Strat purists consider this unsightly. The signature Gilmour tone is provided by a set of prototype pickups from an American Standard Stratocaster, based on an early 1950s model.

A feature that many Stratocaster fans will welcome is that it has been fitted with a shortened tremolo arm.

This makes it easier to add tremolo than is possible with a standard-length arm and helps provide the trademark Gilmour sound.

The Gilmour Stratocaster is definitely a cut above, even by the standard of the other signature models, and has been an instant success. It comes complete with an Evidence audio cable of exactly the same type as Gilmour uses live to achieve crystal clear tone from his guitar. This is an expensive but worthwhile inclusion. The Gilmour Stratocaster is by no means cheap but it is an excellent guitar and one to aspire to.

Many Stratocaster fans had been hoping that the signature model, when it finally appeared, would have been based on a completely different Stratocaster owned by Gilmour, one built in 1954 and bearing the serial number 0001.

David Gilmour owns an extensive collection of between 400 and 500 guitars, including what is possibly the rarest Stratocaster in the world. This was originally made especially for Leo Fender. It was given to Seymour Duncan in the early 1970s and has since passed hands for as little as $900. It eventually came to Phil Taylor, Gilmour's technician. When he needed to borrow some money to buy a house, Gilmour exerted a little blackmail and agreed to lend the money as long as he could buy the 0001 Stratocaster.

The guitar itself is not actually the first Fender Stratocaster made, but it is as close as it gets since the neck plate bears the serial number 0001. The neck is signed in pencil by Taddeo Gomez and dated June 1954, while the body is dated September 1954. The guitar features an early gold anodized pickguard, along with gold hardware and a blonde/white body. It may not necessarily be the earliest of all Stratocasters, but this guitar has lasted for well over fifty years and can still give pleasure at Wembley and in other great stadiums.

# THE CURRENT FENDER STRATOCASTER

The Fender Stratocaster as produced today was first conceived in the early 1980s and named the American Standard Stratocaster. These guitars were aimed directly at professional and working guitarists who weren't happy with the previous CBS instruments. Their loathing for large headstock Stratocasters with sloppy finishes and three-bolt necks had become common knowledge. Fender aimed to set the record straight by releasing a Stratocaster that would feature all the best bits of a classic 1950s or 1960s model, together with improvements to parts that, while not badly made or faulty, could have been made that little bit better.

The American Standard Stratocaster is the staple tool for many guitar players. It is an object of desire in its own right and never has the word standard been so true. The American Standard made its debut at the National Association of Music Merchants (NAMM) show in 1987. The earliest samples of the guitar, however, may be dated back via shipping records to November 1986. The overall concept of the American Standard was a direct first step following the buyout from CBS in 1985, intended to put right everything that had gone wrong in the past fifteen years.

During 1981 Dan Smith had decided to reinvent the Stratocaster and came up with a few changes that still weren't quite right. Bill Schultz, who had himself been a Stratocaster player in his younger days, formed part of a team to build and perfect the Stratocaster and put it straight back into the spotlight.

The Stratocaster's 1980s image was already being further tarnished by the introduction of the Walnut and Strat models. These are not considered among Fender's better products in the 1980s! The Strat was an ugly looking machine in garish colours, albeit with a matching headstock finish and gold-plated hard-ware all over, including the once white plastic knobs. The Walnut Strat was a similar beast in the sense of looking like a walnut. It had all the same features but was made entirely out of dense, heavy black walnut, the only advantage to which was increased sustain. The Walnut Stratocaster was fortunately short-lived due to its non-Stratocaster feature of added weight. Decals of this period simply read 'Fender Strat'.

The idea for a complete Stratocaster revival could easily go down as possibly the saving grace of the Stratocaster and Fender in the 1980s.

## 1st Run American Standard Stratocaster

The first American Standards were displayed at NAMM 1987, with Eric Johnson demonstrating their full potential. Texas-born Eric Johnson has been a fantastic addition to the Stratocaster's ever growing list of players. His own brand of shred and blues rock has catapulted him to worldwide fame. He has been honoured with his own signature model Fender Stratocaster, which is currently one of Fender's best-selling guitars.

The American Standard that hit the shops in 1987 was a truly revolutionary piece of equipment for its time. The guitar approached perfection and would do an excellent job of converting players who had abandoned their Strats in the 1970s in despair at the state of Fender's products. The guitars were available with either maple or rosewood fretboard and in six different finishes: black, sunburst, white, red, blue and, oddly, dark brown. Another feature of the American Standard was its two-point tremolo, which stood firmly on the Stratocaster until 2007, when it was changed for a slightly different design. The tremolo is also a revolutionary part of the Stratocaster's development throughout the years. The original tremolos are great units, but have been loved or loathed for many years, hence the Floyd Rose invasion. I have found that the old tremolos can be fantastic when set up perfectly, but other players have had tuning difficulties that are easily linked to the originals. The original tremolo, with its separate block attached to the body by six screws, was home to six individually adjustable saddles constructed from pressed and bent steel stamped with a small 'Fender Pat. Pend' (or 'Fender Fender' in later years). These bridges were secured at the rear with tension springs. The 1st run American Standard Stratocasters featured the introduction of the two-point tremolo, which meant that the six screws were turned into two solid posts that sat at either edge of the bridge plate and were balanced on a knife-edge fulcrum with the bridge base plate. This gave the tremolo effect a much easier and incredibly smooth action. The same principle applied to the American Standard's rear, which was secured by the classic claw and spring mechanism. This was altered slightly, however, with the springs, made of a lighter gauge, finished in a soft black paint. The springs have been a great success for Fender and are still in use. They are not dissimilar to Floyd Rose tremolo springs, which are again slightly softer when in use.

The saddles of the 1st run American Standard Stratocaster were also revolutionary. They were no longer made from pressed steel but were now thicker and sturdier; this added more mass and hence more tone and sustain. Grub screws greatly improved adjusting the action for perfect intonation (owners everywhere know how difficult it is to adjust the action on old Stratocasters with an Allen key that somehow is never there when you need it). The finish on the saddles is matt, similar to that of graphite. It is known as 'powdered' and is created by forcing powdered metal under very high pressure, while liquid steel would be put in a cast and bent to shape. The powdered steel saddles take out a little bit of the

treble from a Stratocaster but replace it with more sustain and tone.

The electrics on the 1st run American Standard Stratocaster were not too different to those of a 1970s Stratocaster, featuring all the same great characteristics: three pickups, one volume and two tone controls. The pickups, however, now sported flush magnet pole pieces. A five-way switch, as had been added to late 1970s Fender Stratocasters, was fitted as standard. The plastic-coated wire used was basically a cost-saving strategy, since it did the same job at the same level as the expensive cloth-covered wire, but without the aesthetics of vintage feel. All the electrics were mounted on a three-ply pickguard, which Fender has not upgraded since 1959. The guitars have a reverse polarity pickup placed in the middle position; this was to give players a great out-of-phase tone and is the archetypal tone of the 1980s. The TBX (Treble Bass Expander) tone circuit fitted has also stood the test of time since its introduction and is a firm favourite of Eric Clapton. This revolutionary piece of kit makes it possible to completely take out harsh treble frequencies produced by the circuit. Reversing the control reinstalls the treble to please vintage Stratocaster tone purists. The TBX tone control has a midway click that indicates the position and helps the player adjust the Stratocaster's pickup configuration to find his or her ideal tone.

It should be noted that the 1st run American Standard Stratocaster has an older brother that not only helped inspire the Standard but also acted as a kind of surrogate organ donor for parts. The Elite Stratocaster had both good and bad points. It featured an obscure top-loaded tremolo system that was ill received by players due to looks and use. It also featured a Bi-Flex truss rod, TBX tone circuits and a MDX mid-range boost for emulating humbucking style pickups, which have always been a favourite with guitarists worldwide. The Elite Stratocaster changed the appearance of the humble Stratocaster by removing the front-mounted input jack and changed it for a Telecaster-style jack on the bottom right-hand side of the body. The neck grew from the Fender standard radius of 7.14in (18.14cm) to 12in (30.48cm). It also featured single-coil pickups that had no visible pole pieces, but each pickup had its own on/off switch for hum cancelling and tighter tone. The tremolo itself was a snap-on, and short-lived, 'Torq Master' type. The bridge was known as the 'Free Flyte' type, with its snap-on arm and top-loading 'drop-in' stringing. The original idea for electronics for the Elite was to have EMG create a circuit with the mid boosts and high-powered pickups for which the company became famous; David Gilmour of Pink Floyd used an EMG active circuit on his Candy Apple Red 1957 reissue Stratocaster throughout the 1980s and 1990s. The Fender/EMG connection did not materialize in time to meet the Elite Stratocaster's release date, so the circuit was eventually created by Roger Cox, Paul Guegan and Bob Eggler. They also created the three on/off switches for each pickup, mounted with white buttons to the pickguard. The knobs on the Elite had a slight facelift, too, remedying a problem that never actually existed for most players. The knobs had a tight black rubber insert in the side of the skirt. This ran round the whole knob and gave a better grip, but was costly and pointless. If you watch live footage of Rory Gallagher you will notice that his 1961 Stratocaster, even after years and years of heavy use, still worked fine for the violin-style volume swells he became so famous for. The Elite Stratocaster was announced in May 1983, but over the years has become one of Fender's forgotten instruments. It was also flashy and expensive, which ultimately is not what appealed to so many about the Stratocaster, its affordability.

Parts 'borrowed' from the Elite that ended up on the 1st run American Standard Stratocaster included the successful Bi-flex truss rod, which meant that the neck could be easily adjusted in either a convex or concave direction. This design, the brainchild of Charlie Gresset at Fender, has become a firm favourite of many players over the years. The Schaller locking-type strap buttons were also borrowed (a valuable addition, since I'm sure many players have experienced seeing their beloved Stratocaster hit the floor with great force). The tuners are Schaller-made and Fender-branded sealed units with a high ratio; they are well made and offer little or no friction. The last component to be carried over to the 1st run American Standard was the Ezy-Glyder string trees, which offer very little friction on the G and D string, as well as on the B and E, and keep the string firmly in the nut during heavy-handed playing. Luckily the 12in radius didn't stay and was replaced by a Fender-user friendly 9.5in (24.1cm). The new neck was not favoured by Gibson players who were happy with the opposite arrangement, a classic case of not pleasing everyone!

The 1st run American Standard was designed to be cost-effective and well-made. It also exceeded expectations as a players' guitar with customizable options such as the 'swimming pool' route underneath the pickguard, which enabled the player to add a pickup configuration such as dual humbuckers or a humbucker and two single coils; providing you had the money, anything was possible. The body was finished in a thick polyurethane paint with a polyester undercoat, which meant that battered 'undesirable' Stratocasters were now a thing of the past. How wrong they were. The body wood used on American Standards was alder until 1990, when that wood became in short supply and Fender was forced to use poplar for about three years. Although poplar is generally not used for tone, James Burton is a big fan and it is used on his signature Telecaster, which has been a top-selling Fender since its introduction in 1990.

The headstock logo on the 1st run American Standard Stratocasters was modelled on the 'Transition' period logo of 1965; it was altered slightly with the lettering in silver instead of gold, and the serial number was placed below. It also made its model name clear by having 'Made in USA' set below 'Stratocaster'.

The 1st runs were packed into form-fit ABS plastic flight cases, which many consider the best cases for a gigging musician. Further small improvements included twenty-two frets and the well-received micro-tilt adjustment on the neck plate, which eliminated any need for shimming. These guitars measure up nicely as a good all-rounder.

The 1st run American Standard Stratocasters were a groundbreaking development that, depending on condition, should potentially be high-grade investments in years to come. They are not perfect but they have proved their quality throughout the years.

## 2nd Run American Standard Stratocaster

No further alterations were made to the American Standard Stratocaster until 1995–96. These resulted in what is in effect the 2nd run. The main features were a different tone circuit affectionately known as the Delta Tone, which basically acted like a TBX control but was a 'no load'. Whereas the notch on the TBX control was halfway, the Delta Tone would cut itself out of the circuit at 10, so giving the pickups a wide tone with no tone control; with the Delta Tone you hear the pickup on its own and without interference.

The guitars from this run were shipped out with the first examples of the Hot Rod series Stratocasters. These are technically American Standards with upgraded pickups: the Lonestar Stratocaster incorporated a Seymour Duncan Pearly Gates humbucker in the bridge position; the Roadhouse Stratocaster had three Texas special single coils; and the Big Apple Stratocaster was fitted with two humbuckers. In order to advertise their Hot Rod roots, they were fitted with a tortoiseshell (Roadhouse) or pearloid (Big Apple and Lonestar) pickguard. Included in the price were three paint finishes not otherwise available on the American Standard: Shoreline Gold, silver and metallic.

The logo had a quick revamp, too. The transitional logo that had lasted since the first American Standards was dropped and replaced with a silver spaghetti logo, which also had 'Made in USA' below it. The guitars were unchanged apart from these slight modifications, leading to media criticism in the UK that not enough had been changed. For many guitar players, however, the 2nd run American Standard was the calm before the storm.

## 3rd Run American Standard Stratocaster

The dawn of the new millennium bought many changes to guitar players around the world, especially those who base their whole sound around the

Fender Stratocaster. The stock Fender USA Standard Stratocaster was becoming slightly dated when set against Fender's other guitars, such as the Custom Shop Stratocasters, Signature models and Vintage reissues. These guitars had all been very successful in appealing to guitar players who love the feel of old instruments, the signature sound of particular artists or just the pure luxury of having a custom-made instrument, which for many is the pinnacle of instrument ownership. A Fender USA Standard Stratocaster from either the first or second run did not stand well next to a precision-engineered '57 Stratocaster or the Stevie Ray Vaughan Stratocaster. It lacks vintage charm, feel and, above all, tone. Fender decided to make what can only be described as the finest and best-manufactured Stratocaster offered for less than £1,000. The guitar not only had a facelift cosmetically but received some minor fine tuning that, to many, made all the difference.

The first change made in 2000 was to give a body option of alder or ash, owing to the ever-increasing demand in the guitar media for tone. It seemed then that all guitar players wanted was a decent tone, good woods, good pickups and great playability. Having a bulging wallet will always buy you a fine tone, but Fender realized that there are players who can't afford dream machines from the Custom Shop but are perfectly capable of making a great tone from guitars that don't have to cost the earth. The 3rd run American Standard Stratocaster was the perfect solution.

Over the years the 2nd run American Standard Stratocaster had managed to look slightly chunky and less ergonomic than vintage models or even reissues. The first problem to be solved was that the body had to be more rounded and sleek, so that the design could hark back to the original body shape and feel great on the player. The contour became deeper again, the overall thickness was reduced and the now undesirable 'swimming pool' rout was dropped. Players had decided that the large rout was completely functional but gave the 1st and 2nd run Standards a slightly hollow tone that was great for some but loathed by many. The 3rd run Stratocaster decided to pick a different rout that would enable the most practical pickup configuration but wouldn't sacrifice any wood that didn't need to be sacrificed. The final rout chosen ended up as HSH, which means you can have a Humbucker in the bridge, a single coil in the middle or a Humbucker in the neck. Standard Stratocasters came complete with three single coils in the HSH rout for any players that wanted to tinker with the electrics. All you need is a soldering iron, a replacement pickguard, humbuckers, patience and a steady hand.

The new bodies had a touch more weight but a lot more tone. All the mid-range frequencies came together, the bass was deeper and the trebles were perfect. The alder was not veneered, which had been a small issue in previous Stratocasters. With all the pieces in place the body was ready for action.

The electrics were also tightened up on the 3rd run. The Delta Tone from the last update stayed put as there had been no complaints. The flush magnets produced a relatively flat tone that inspired plenty of modifications. The replacement pickup units boasted higher output, heavier tone and also brought the famous staggered pole piece magnets, for which many great Stratocasters have been so popular. The pickups in the new bodies were a great match for the gigging musician.

The neck received the biggest and most noticeable changes on the 3rd run American Standard. The neck on earlier models was relatively flat and felt quite mass-manufactured to most players. The 3rd run inspired the Fender team to make it feel good in the palm of the player's hand. The necks were previously finished in polyester, which feels very manufactured and plastic-like, but the new necks were finished lightly with an eggshell/matte finish, which prevents sticky build-ups of skin and sweat. The new finish allows someone to play all night and not worry about having to clean the rear of the neck. This proved an instant success. The frets on previous Stratocaster models had always felt as if the guitar had just come direct from the factory. This was not a problem to some, but many found it slightly uncomfortable for the first few years until the frets were worn in on the edges. Fender listened to the players' pleas and every neck was now hand rolled so that it felt 'broken in'. The concept is similar to that of worn jeans, which always fit better.

The other change came with staggered machine heads. The headstock on an old 1950s or 1960s Stratocaster is timeless, simple and uncluttered. The previous American Standards, however, had a lot going on: big tuning posts, two string trees, a Bi-Flex truss rod adjuster and a thick logo, which was eventually changed but still left the remaining parts.

The headstock on the 3rd run lost its tuners in favour of the Schaller staggered variety, meaning that the first E A D string posts were shorter than the next G B E tuners. This was done solely to eliminate the second string tree, which had been introduced in the mid-1970s and stayed ever since on the headstock. Having one string tree instead of two removed a lot of friction in the tuning. The posts were manufactured with a suitable groove built in, which keeps the string pulled down over the nut and gives a better angle, similar to that of a Gibson Les Paul or SG, without the need for an angled headstock. The Bi-Flex truss rod adjuster remained.

One small change was made to the cosmetic appearance of the headstock. For the 3rd run, Fender retained the silver spaghetti logo but incorporated the long-lost 'Original Contour Body' decal that had been removed from Stratocasters in the 1970s. With that in place the 3rd run American Standard Stratocaster was perfection.

The guitar's overall shape during the 3rd run was perfect, so much so that Fender went with slightly different cosmetics for the pickguards and plastics. In previous runs these had been brilliant white, which few players favoured. The new Stratocaster had parchment-coloured parts, an ever so slightly off-white finish that appealed to many players. The guitar came in its form-fit case in a rainbow of Fender's finest colours, including Hot Rod Red, Aquamarine Blue, black, blonde, white and three-colour sunburst.

During this period Fender decided to make their new better sounding and better playing guitar known and accessible to all players and tastes. The new models that came out alongside the Standard Stratocaster featured all the popular modifications that players opted for and are affectionately known as the Hot Rod series: the American Fat Strat Texas Special, the American Double Fat Strat and the American Texas

Special Strat. All of these guitars worked on the basic principle that they were American Standards but were equipped with a Texas Special pickup (Texas Special Strat), a humbucker with two Texas Specials (Fat Strat Texas Special) or two humbuckers (Double Fat Strat). They were upgraded Hot Rod models from the 2nd run, and were effectively the same bar the name change.

## 4th Run Fender American Standard Stratocaster

When Fender decided to revamp the American Standard Stratocaster one more time, eyebrows were raised all over the world as players wondered what needed improving, since many thought the previous run had been perfection. The new model arrived in early 2008 and was promoted as part of the 'Make History' campaign. The changes to the Stratocaster had been mainly cosmetic. There is not a lot to separate the two runs. The newer model has done away with the powdered steel bridge, which was in the process of becoming a classic. Instead there is what is claimed to be the best of both worlds:  the two-point base plate, but using steel saddles identical to those used on reissues and original specification models. One reviewer, however, has said that these saddles are prone to string slippage as well as loss of overall tone.

One other alteration was the addition of a gloss lacquer-finished headstock face, which means that the neck stayed identical to the 3rd run but the front of the headstock is gloss finished. This little adjustment could be credited to John Mayer, as his signature model incorporated this feature in years previous. The fingerboard on maple-necked Stratocasters in the 4th run has been fully lacquered. This small improvement allows the look of a maple-neck Stratocaster to remain in good condition longer, which may be a questionable feature given the popularity of Relic guitars. The actual lacquer used is slightly darker, since a few players had mentioned that the previous runs had slightly pale-looking maple necks that varied from model to model.

Instead of a moulded Fender flight case, which many players appreciated for its size and weight, the 4th run American Standard comes complete with an oblong SKB flight case. While some feel that this is a slight letdown, since it is not as ergonomic as the previous case, it does however provide more space for accessories such as straps, leads, plectrums and strings.

# STRATOCASTERS BACK FROM THE FUTURE

Many players and guitar enthusiasts claim that the first time they saw a real Fender Stratocaster they thought it looked highly futuristic or like something from outer space. So it is only fitting that Fender should move with the times in order to keep the Stratocaster and its features from becoming stale. The Fender design team has come up with two very different concepts that, while offering a great all-purpose guitar for the gigging musician and a good all-round Stratocaster, were intended to change the way guitar players adopted the Stratocaster.

## Roland Ready Stratocaster

During the mid-1990s guitar players worldwide were seeking a new type of sound to complement the electro and dance music that was currently invading the airwaves of many radio stations. Players were soon plugging their guitars into computers or laptops in the search for new tones and sounds. It seemed that computers were the only resource left, since many players thought that foot-controlled effects pedals had reached their limits as far as quality and tone went.

Fender decided to make life easier for players who wished to use these alternative effects and made a deal with Roland Electronics from Japan. The result was the Roland Ready Stratocaster, a standard, no frills, Mexican-built Stratocaster available in black, white or sunburst. What set it apart – and it was not everyone's cup of tea – was the Roland GK-2A pickup below the bridge that nearly doubled the price of a Mexican standard Stratocaster, The new guitar did, however, save a lot of time for anyone who wanted

a computer-compatible pickup but could not find a repairman brave enough to fit the unit.

The GK-2A pickup was a complex piece of kit and required extra routing, complex wiring and, above all else, patience. The pickup itself runs on separate batteries for its power. This put off many Stratocaster fans as it detracts from the original idea of a working man's guitar, since you shouldn't need to put batteries in your tools. The Roland Ready Stratocaster arrived around 1995 and allowed some tech-happy guitar players to breathe a sigh of relief at a standard Stratocaster fitted with the GK-2A pickup. This allowed the player to create synthesizer sounds, flute sounds and ring modulator sounds at the flick of a switch. The pickup also worked well with a foot controller for live use.

The Stratocaster had now moved into the 1990s. The new pickup addition took the hassle out of fitting one and learning how to adjust to its use; players could now just try one and decide. Before the introduction of the Roland Ready Stratocaster the pickup had been extensively used by Ritchie Blackmore and it is now a standard feature on his Custom Shop models. When fitted separately the pickup unit is unsightly as the main unit sits on the body and numerous leads have to be plugged in connecting it to the guitar and foot pedal, if required. On the Roland Ready Stratocaster this was already installed into the guitar's pickup cavities and the controls mounted to the pickguard. This made the guitar much less unsightly than one that had been adapted to take the pickup.

The Roland Ready Stratocaster also incorporated MIDI technology so that players could upload files to their computers safely and securely. The settings could then be saved ready for use for gigs or recordings, hence the guitar's brand name.

The Roland Ready Stratocaster has remained in the Fender catalogue and the original design was upgraded after the development of the VG Stratocaster (*see below*). The current Roland Ready Stratocaster uses a comfortable 9.5in (24.1cm) radius neck and three standard Mexican Stratocaster single-coil pickups. Twenty-one medium jumbo frets are fitted. The guitar has everything necessary to make a Stratocaster comfortable in the player's hands.

The electrics fitted incorporate two push switches enabling the onboard synthesizer effects to be quickly switched on or off. The addition of a three-way toggle switch allows a combination of the Stratocaster's standard pickups with the Roland unit. The switching mechanism retained the standard five-way switching for when the player got tired of synthesizer sounds or, quite possibly, the batteries died mid-take or mid-set!

The Roland Ready Stratocaster is an interesting part of the brand's history. This was the first time Fender had used synthesizer technology on its guitars. It was also at a price that many could afford; if the pickup had been added to an American Stratocaster the retail price could have been much higher. The cost, build, features and the inclusion of a free gig bag have done the Roland Ready Stratocaster many favours throughout the years, even though its current habitat is the standard pages of the humble Mexican Stratocaster range.

## Fender/Roland VG Stratocaster

The VG Stratocaster is a slightly more user-friendly guitar that hit the shelves in mid-2007. It upped the stakes and was billed as the only guitar you'd ever need. Based on an American Standard Stratocaster, this guitar opened up endless possibilities using a control knob (a little shorter and smaller than a standard knob) that allows the player to choose a Stratocaster sound or that of a Telecaster, Les Paul or acoustic, all which are all available through the inclusion of the Roland VG pickup.

The VG ('virtual guitar') pickup carries the string sensor, which receives a signal from whatever the player does and digitally transforms it into an artificial guitar sound ready to come out through any amplification. The second tone knob allows the player to select any type of tuning he desires: options on the VG Stratocaster are normal, drop D, open G, D modal, twelve-string and drop B tuning. These selections are marked on the knob as T for tuning and the modelling knob is depicted with M. The controls are matched with a master volume for all settings and a master tone control.

The only drawback to the VG Stratocaster is that it enjoys its batteries: the guitar would get only a few weeks' use out of them, depending on the brand, and gigging musicians found this off-putting.

Despite this, the VG Stratocaster has many strong points. The guitar has more class than the Roland Ready Stratocaster as it incorporates Roland's finest virtual guitar technology into Fender's best-selling Stratocaster line. The VG Stratocaster is certainly a milestone as it demonstrates Fender's ability to keep up with the latest developments and technologies. The guitar comes in black or sunburst, with either a maple or rosewood fretboard and medium jumbo frets.

The build quality is also superb, with neat routings, clean finishes and professionally fitted electronics with an easy-use battery compartment in the guitar's rear. The VG received mixed reviews when it reached guitar shops worldwide. Its saving grace was that there was no provision for storing settings in banks, which when used in a pedal format or MIDI file could have caused chaos for the player. Instead the VG Stratocaster allowed the player to select the model and tuning, and then just play. This simplicity was well received.

The layout of the VG Stratocaster differs from the Roland Ready Stratocaster in that there is a small bright blue LED next to the master volume to indicate when the guitar is in digital mode. American Standard pickups, operated by a five-way switch, are included for when the player wants regular Stratocaster sounds or when the batteries fail. Elsewhere on the guitar the components are identical to the ones used on the popular American Standard Stratocaster design from 2000 to 2007. And so it was that Fender went digital.

# Reasoning

It might seem strange that a company like Fender, which has been rooted in the originality of their guitars, should keep on adding futuristic features such as synthesizer pickups and modelling units to classic designs such as like the Stratocaster.

The VG Stratocaster was seemingly developed to compete with the Variax guitar, the brainchild of the Line 6 design team from Japan. Line 6, which originally manufactured amplifiers and effects units, struck gold with the POD unit, a device allowing players to simulate any amplifier they wish, and to add and remove effects at the touch of a button. The POD unit and Spider amplifier (incorporating effects and amplifiers into a small combo amplifier) have had huge success and the company has a reputation for creating good tones that don't sound too artificial. The next step was to create the Variax, an instrument with its own different guitar sounds and tones built in. The Variax hit the market in the early 2000s and was immediately popular with players and musicians, receiving great reviews. Just as with a VG Stratocaster, the Variax uses different models of guitar in its design and allows players to use a humbucker-equipped guitar sound and then, with a quick turn of a pot, switch the tone to acoustic. The great disadvantage of such technologically advanced guitars, however, is that should your VG Stratocaster or Variax cease to work it must be flown straight back to America or Japan to be rectified, since very few know how or get enough practice on digital guitars to be able to carry out necessary repairs.

It is to be hoped that the next fifty years won't see Fender doing away with the Stratocaster in its original format or come to think of it as just a few solder joints, screws and springs with some nice bits of timber and paint. The digital age has transformed life when applied to computers, mobile phones and media devices, but perhaps it has not been so successful when applied to an instrument that requires creativity and originality to perform well. The next digital advance is always just around the corner. Priced at more than £1,500, the VG Stratocaster doesn't make life much easier for the guitar player, when for that same basic budget you could easily afford a good Stratocaster, a large effects unit and a valve amplifier. The VG Stratocaster is an interesting guitar to inspect and play, but many feel that it will become dated very quickly in the current technological race, especially now that Gibson has developed a digital Les Paul and a self-tuning range of guitars.

# NOTABLE STRATOCASTER LISTENING

Many recordings feature the Stratocaster in full cry. The following selection of artists and albums will enable you to hear a broad spectrum of players as well as their specific Stratocasters. Where possible I have also listed the amplifiers used, as this should give some idea of how this also reflects their individual tone.

I hope this will inspire those with a strong interest in all types of music to explore the capabilities of the Stratocaster.

## Jimi Hendrix

As with all things Stratocaster, Hendrix is never far away in conversation. His use of a Stratocaster in all his recorded work is regarded by many as the pinnacle of electric guitar playing.

*Are You Experienced* (1967)

His first album, *Are You Experienced*, was an instant hit. It was recorded through his newly acquired 100w Marshall stack (1959slp 100w with two 4 × 12in cabinets). The overall tone throughout the album is not quite as full as his later work, but still retains guitar genius and an awesome Stratocaster quality. *Are You*

*Experienced* is a fast-paced rock album that showcases Hendrix as a blues, rock and soulful guitar player.

*Axis: Bold as Love* (1967)

Hendrix's second album, *Axis: Bold as Love*, was released at the end of 1967. It allowed Hendrix to add a little more jazz to his style. The Stratocaster is predominant throughout the whole album. During 'Little Wing' Hendrix utilizes the out-of-phase sound achieved by lodging the then three-way switch with cardboard or some other suitable material. The album is again a must for anyone interested in the real sound of a Fender Stratocaster. The album's intro is interesting as it features Hendrix pushing his Stratocaster into a max volume Marshall Stack to achieve severe feedback with a wah wah pedal plugged in backwards.

*Electric Ladyland* (1968)

*Electric Ladyland* is a slightly more adventurous album with Hendrix using various types of guitar on single tracks. This is the album that has the iconic 'Voodoo Chile (Slight Return)' as the final track, in which Hendrix uses his Stratocaster and wah-wah pedal together to create possibly one of the best intros of all time, combining muted strings and odd rhythms in an effect that could only have been made with a Stratocaster. The same track also features Hendrix playing the three-way switch on his Stratocaster to create a tone that simulates a slight stereo effect on one note. This is an album that Stratocaster fans should definitely own.

*Woodstock* (1969)

*Band of Gypsys* (1970)

*Woodstock* and *Band of Gypsys* showcase two famous Hendrix Stratocasters. The Woodstock Stratocaster seemed to have a very bright tone, which at some points in the recording sounds quite hollow, but it must also be noted that these are both live albums so they should not be judged strictly on the overall sound. They are, however, great albums to experience the 'master of the Stratocaster' at work with no overdubs or fancy studio effects. Listening to *Woodstock* on your own at full volume is an enlightening experience. *Band of Gypsys* on the other hand is a very heavy and yet soulful album. Owing to a recording contract

dispute that came back to haunt Hendrix, the rhythm section on *Band of Gypsys* was altered to suit Buddy Miles and Billy Cox. Although the album was not liked by many Hendrix fans, it has some of the best live Hendrix work ever recorded and is held in high regard by such players as Joe Satriani, Stone Gossard and Rich Robinson of the Black Crowes. You can hear the black 1968 Stratocaster in full flight here as Hendrix tears the Fillmore East apart in the epic performance of 'Machine Gun' in protest at the Vietnam war. As on the infamous 'Star Spangled Banner' at Woodstock, the track shows much abuse can be given to a Stratocaster while it still vaguely retains its concert pitch tuning.

## Eric Clapton

An early Gibson player throughout his early career with John Mayall and Cream, Eric Clapton picked up the Stratocaster seemingly when Hendrix died in 1970. Throughout the 1970s Clapton used his beloved 'Blackie' Stratocaster to record interesting blends of reggae, southern rock and soft rock, genres of music that had never before been attempted by a 'blues' guitar player. The two albums featured here display Clapton's prowess in the genres.

*461 Ocean Boulevard* (1974)

*461 Ocean Boulevard*, then Clapton's address on Golden Beach, Miami, shows him to be a skilled reggae musician, incorporating the Stratocaster into the style. The tones heard on *461* are that of 'Blackie' playing through a small Fender Champ amplifier. This is the sound that Fender fans aim for when recording their own music.

*Layla and Other Assorted Love Songs*
(Derek and the Dominos, 1970)

'Layla', Clapton's all-time classic, has a beautiful ending enhanced by the legendary Duane Allman. It is great to hear the tone of Allman's Les Paul against 'Brownie', a 1956 sunburst Stratocaster Clapton employed here as a substitute for 'Blackie'. The sound of the two guitars in unison is the stuff of legend. The tones heard from Clapton's Stratocaster are those of distinction; the Fender Stratocaster and Fender amplifier had never before met so graciously on a recording.

## Stevie Ray Vaughan

*Texas Flood* (1983)

*Couldn't Stand the Weather* (1984)

SRV, as he is abbreviated, was one of Texas's finest exports. His blend of blues, rock and swing music can be heard to new heights on *Texas Flood*. The whole album is archetypal Stratocaster from start to finish, showcasing numerous Stratocaster tones. SRV was famous for using the bridge and middle position tone on his Stratocaster, which allowed a hollow tone that was inevitably beefed up by Vaughan's desire for volume and heavy strings tuned low. This resulted in a overwhelming Stratocaster 'on steroids' tone that exploded onto the guitar world. (It should also be noted that a young Stevie Ray Vaughan, playing a heavy Stratocaster solo, is featured towards the end of David Bowie's hit 'Let's Dance'. This was Vaughan's first break and by no means his last.)

*Couldn't Stand the Weather* is another Strat-fest that contains some of Vaughan's finest work. The album includes a cover of 'Voodoo Chile' that incorporates all the Stratocaster tricks that Hendrix used years before.

## Hank Marvin

Released on Columbia Records, this album shows off very early UK Stratocaster playing. It features Hank Marvin playing a brand new Stratocaster (1959) through a Vox AC30 and provides some of the cleanest Stratocaster playing known. The cover of the album depicts Hank and the Shadows casually clutching their instruments. The album, which features a cover of Santo and Johnny's 'Sleepwalk', where Hank makes good use of his Stratocaster's tremolo arm, is very easy to listen to, something that makes a change from many guitar-based albums. The Shadows inspired an awful lot of great guitar players like Mark Knopfler, Brian May and Chris Rea, and every Stratocaster fan should have at least one Shadows album in their collection.

## Tom Morello

*Rage Against the Machine* (1992)

*Renegades* (2000)

Many do not consider Morello as the ideal Stratocaster hero as his heavily modified Stratocasters are usually covered in graffiti. Throughout his time with Rage Against the Machine he used mainly Stratocaster copies or cheaper Japanese Fenders. The interesting point about Morello's tone is that his Stratocasters are usually equipped with humbuckers that give an intriguing tone, quite open sounding with a lot of force when volume is applied, somewhere between a Gibson and a Fender. His use of a modified Stratocaster on his band's eponymous album is a landmark recording for it stretched the possibilities of what can be done to a Stratocaster with a soldering iron, router and a steady hand. Morello pushed the Stratocaster as far as it could possibly go both physically and in recording terms.

*Renegades* is an interesting follow-up showcasing Morello's use of a Stratocaster and numerous effects to achieve rock, funk and even hip hop effects (for example on the cover of Cypress Hill's 'How I could just kill a man'). These are two albums are definitely worth a listen. They define a decade when the Stratocaster was less in favour than guitars such as the Ibanez RG series.

## Billy Corgan

*Mellon Collie and the Infinite Sadness* (1995)

Smashing Pumpkins front man/guitarist Corgan has been honoured with a signature Stratocaster following a series of big-selling albums. The tone with which he is now associated, known as the 'buzz-saw', comes from Corgan using his 1970s Stratocaster to push as much gain into his sound as it will take, so achieving a distinctive sawing tone that retained the guitar's clarity as well as making a groundbreaking tone never heard before.

The sounds achieved and Corgan's unique playing style have gained legendary status.

## Adrian Smith

*The Number of the Beast* (1982)

Iron Maiden rose to fame as part of the heavy metal genre explosion in the early 1980s. Guitarists Adrian Smith and Janick Gers are both Stratocaster devotees (one of Smith's formerly belonged to the late, great Paul Kossoff). The mixture of tones heard on this album, based on a humbucking Stratocaster pickup with a Floyd Rose tremolo fitted, sum up the heavy metal Stratocaster ethos. The result is an impressive brew of dive bombs mixed with pinched harmonics, and even though most guitar players either love or hate it, the talent and musicianship should be appreciated. The Stratocaster is present in the majority of Maiden's recordings. The album is a landmark both for heavy metal and for the Stratocaster.

## John Mayer

*Try!* (John Mayer Trio, 2005)

This seminal live album has the pop prince from Connecticut turn his back on pop music and plunge head first into blues rock. Armed with a Custom Shop Stratocaster, Mayer utilizes all the Stratocaster's features from the tremolo, pickups and even behind the nut for bends. The playing on the album is second to none. Tone-wise it is mainly the neck pickup or the middle and bridge, reflecting Mayer's love of SRV's playing and tone.

The cover of Hendrix's 'Wait Until Tomorrow' features some incredibly good guitar playing in what is possibly one of the thickest Stratocaster tones ever

heard. This is coupled with a modified Blues Driver pedal into a Vibroverb amplifier. This combination would normally bring a cleaner Fender tone, but with Mayer the tone is second to none and the guitar playing is first class. Anyone with an interest in guitar playing should listen to this album and marvel at the quality of the tone achieved.

## Robin Trower

*Bridge of Sighs* (1974)

A classic 1970s album in its own right, this album has divided opinions since many consider Trower to be a 'Hendrix clone'. It is true that there are definite similarities between the two, but clone is too strong a term. Trower achieved a much thicker Stratocaster tone than Hendrix on recordings. The use of a Uni-Vibe is evident on several tracks on this album, but it is interesting to hear such a smooth and fluid player with a Stratocaster. For much of the 1970s Trower used early 1950s models, whereas Hendrix preferred shiny, new models from the 1960s. Early 1950s Stratocasters have a tone of their own and these are the guitars, of which Trower had many, that are heard on this album. The results are unique and quite heavy, but it is still blatantly a Stratocaster sound throughout. The album is a winner and great played very loud. *Guitarist* magazine once referred to Trower's tone as 'milkshake thick' and no better description has ever been applied to Trower or this album.

# FENDER CUSTOM SHOP STRATOCASTERS

The Fender Custom Shop first opened its doors in 1987 and set out to create instruments of the highest calibre. Its magical creations are some of the finest guitars currently available. The Custom Shop, situated in Corona, California, is home to the Time Machine range as well as to many one-off and limited edition guitars. Themes chosen to inspire new models have included psychedelia, Marilyn Monroe, Harley Davidsons, pool tables, Hello Kitty and many more. These guitars are usually sold out instantly. The Custom Shop will design and build pretty much any Stratocaster it can possibly manage. Some of its Stratocasters have sold at auction in excess of £20,000. These guitars are very highly regarded by players and collectors alike.

The Custom Shop is also known for its tribute series of guitars, which are offered in a run usually limited to about fifty or a hundred. These guitars are always highly priced and usually sell out within weeks of being released.

The Fender Custom Shop is also the first port of call for artists who need guitars for upcoming tours, gigs or studio dates. Master builders usually drop everything to work with an artist on a guitar collaboration, which usually results in a highly sought-after and perhaps even iconic instrument.

Builders at the Custom Shop over the years have often been held in such high regard for their skills that they have been able to leave and start up their own successful guitar companies. An example of this is John Suhr, who now owns and runs Suhr Guitars in California. Other notable builders are Jay Black, John English and Mark Kendrick.

Over the last ten years, many guitar companies have added a boutique area to their guitar operations. Gibson, Martin and PRS have all introduced a suc-cessful custom shop-style option for their customers. Fender's Custom Shop was the first to open.

Since the Fender Custom Shop's output of high-grade Stratocasters has been so extensive over more than twenty years, it has been difficult to make a selection for this chapter. I have chosen A selection of future classic custom shop Stratocasters which have been suitably 'relic'ed' to look like older Stratocasters and show all the signs of use.

## Fender Flame Top Stratocaster

This guitar, loosely based upon a 1962 Stratocaster, has the addition of high-grade flame maple to the neck of the guitar and to the guitar's body. It is a desirable guitar finished in three-tone sunburst. However, many purists would not look twice at it due to its non-original finishing; but this adds a twist to a classic guitar that would not normally be present. It also allows the player to have a 'regular' Stratocaster, with the addition of the Custom Shop's finest work incorporated.

The guitar has all the Custom Shop electrics, which will be a good set of CTS pots and a CRL switch wired up with cloth-covered wire. These are all mounted to a standard white pickguard and plastics assembly. The guitar has Custom Shop pickups fitted, which are not year-specific but are designed closely to the 1960s units. This guitar is easily identifiable as a mid '90s build due to its rear headstock logo; older Custom Shop guitars have a distinctive 'F' in the middle as well as 'USA' underneath the Cadillac-inspired logo on the headstock rear.

The guitar's neck features highly-figured flame maple at the rear, as well as high African rosewood. The frets are in keeping with the guitar's vintage styling and smaller vintage frets have been fitted. The other interesting feature that this guitar incorporates is the fully-engraved neck plate, which detracts from its 1960s basis; the neck plate has all the Custom Shop details similar to the headstock rear.

The hardware used on this guitar is in keeping with the 1960s styling, with Gotoh Kluson style machineheads and a vintage bridge assembly. The guitar, due to its year, is housed in a tweed case, which is typical of Fender in the 1990s putting almost all of their guitars into non year-specific cases. This type of Stratocaster, depending on which year of the 1960s it is based on, should have either a blonde or brown Tolex case. This is due to Fender manufacturing their own cases in this period; it could be classed as pre-C+G.

## 1956 Relic, Black over White Stratocaster

These days this is a commonly-seen Stratocaster from the Custom Shop. It is a heavy relic model, and with collectors' tastes expanding all the time, Fender decided to meet demands and make Stratocasters with specific finishes. The flame top Stratocaster above was released at a time when the vintage market was buoyant, with 1960s and 50s Stratocasters for sale all over the world at relatively cheap prices. I remember seeing 1960s Stratocasters for sale in shops at around £2,000 to £3,000. But by 2009, you would be hard-pressed to find a 1960s Stratocaster in a reasonable condition for less than £10,000; mint examples cost in excess of £15,000–£20,000.

The Custom Shop has filled this gap by making replicas of 1950s and 60s guitars. The Stratocaster's cooler users, like John Frusciante, Rory Gallagher and Stevie Ray Vaughan, all used highly-worn and abused models, which have become very fashionable. Hence models like this 1956 Relic, officially classed as a 'heavy relic', show the black finish worn in typical places and exposing a white undercoat. This is now considered a very cool trait in Stratocasters. Originally guitars were finished in a custom colour, such as Sonic Blue, white or Surf Green, but if a last-minute order for a black model came in, and an unsold or back-ordered guitar would be selected and sprayed black. Hopefully the customer would never know what colour his or her guitar was originally. This is now another aspect that appeals to Stratocaster collectors.

This guitar is based upon a 1956 Stratocaster that has been used heavily for years and has its undercoat of white exposed. The guitar has a fantastic build quality and a good set of Custom Shop electrics. This incorporates a set of specially designed 1956 pickups, which have a slightly lower output than many of its contemporaries. This results in a sweet tone that will vary from one guitar to the next. Many agree that there is nothing sweeter than a black Stratocaster with a maple neck; I have to agree whole-heartedly.

The guitar is packaged with a period-correct tweed case and what is known as 'case candy', which means strap, lead, manuals and tags. This guitar also shows its certificate of authenticity, which does add a certain amount of value to a second-hand custom shop instrument.

## Fender 1960 Relic Stratocaster

Here is a great-looking example of a commonly-seen Stratocaster, which also has the reputation of being one of the most boring! The argument against black guitars is that the colour black has been known for thousands of years as being the absence of colour; it can look great on many things, but is also used as a mask for poor workmanship. For example, many cheap Stratocaster copies are finished in black for reasons of making the overall guitar seem like a fine piece of art. However, stripping back the paint will reveal a great magnitude of wood defects; for example, the use of plywood, knots in poor quality timber and even filled cracks in rotten and cured wood. The majority of cheap guitars exported around the world are finished in black, hence their usual asking price of just under

£100. They also generally have poor rosewood added to the maple, as maple necks take a little more work than rosewood with lacquering and finishing. Unfinished maple will get very dirty very quickly; the same is the case with rosewood, of course, but the point is that rosewood is naturally dark.

This guitar has its own vibe, as it is in the least desirable colour scheme. Due to its price and the widespread availability of black Stratocaster-esque guitars, this Stratocaster will be providing its owner with its own piece of great workmanship; the guitar is based on a 1960 Stratocaster in 'custom colour' black. The black finish on a guitar like this is complimented nicely by the dark maple on the headstock front and dark rosewood fretboard. The guarantee of quality with this guitar is its place of manufacture; the wood used is high-grade alder for the neck, and high-grade maple and rosewood for the fretboard.

The overall finish of the guitar has a relic treatment added. This shows relatively light wear and tear, unlike the heavy relic of the 1956 model in this section. The guitar's overall appearance is worn yet done tastefully and shows various knocks and scrapes. The maple on the neck is also treated to the famous vintage tint of the lacquer.

This guitar has closely matched 1960s pickups and electrics, which again will be a lower output and give the guitar its own unique sound. This guitar also has plenty of case candy, with certificate and a period correct brown Tolex case.

## Fender 60 Relic Daphne Blue and Red Sparkle Stratocasters

A collector's dream, the Daphne Blue Fender 60 relic guitar is highly prized by collectors all over the world. The light blue colour that was used in the early 1960s was famously used on John Lennon and George Harrison's Stratocasters, which were purchased by then roadie Mal Evans. When the Fab Four recorded *Rubber Soul*, Harrison's went psychedelic and Lennon's vanished. The Daphne Blue relic guitar is a fine example

of the Custom Shop's excellent ideas when building a collector's piece. This type of guitar in its original form would be worth somewhere in the region of £40,000; a Custom Shop example costs considerably less, but will perform in exactly the same way and possibly be more reliable than an original. This guitar is highly desirable to many players and Stratocaster fans alike.

The Red Sparkle Stratocaster is another fine instrument; this type of guitar is identical to the Daphne Blue model, bar more wear and tear on the paint. The idea behind this was that in the early 1960s, when a player acquired his or her Stratocaster, it would be played constantly, resulting in the amount of wear shown. This is another desirable point to collectors when buying a rare Stratocaster. Worn examples are looking more authentic these days with the amount of faked Stratocasters around.

Both examples are housed in period correct cases with suitable 'candy' included.

## 1969 Relic Stratocaster

With the Custom Shop producing relic guitars, it became apparent that the only late-1960s Stratocaster that would be popular would be a 1969 model, due to the media's heavy coverage of Jimi Hendrix's performances from Woodstock. Because the festival took place in 1969, this meant that customers for a Hendrix-style Stratocaster would want a 1969 model for the added bonus of telling people that they owned a 'Woodstock' Stratocaster. The only actual difference between a 1968 and a 1969 Stratocaster would be the last number in year of manufacture.

The 1969 relic guitar is suitably finished in Olympic White with a worn maple neck. The interesting point to note about this guitar and other relic 1969s is that the finish does not show as much wear on either body or neck, due to the manufacturing differences in the respective year. The late 1960s Stratocasters have polyester overcoats on the entire guitar, making it tougher-wearing and showing less stress in later years. This specific guitar shows wear and tear, but in keeping with the year it is based on, the guitar also shows less wear being technically 'newer' than an early 1960s or 1950s model.

The main reason the Custom Shop added a CBS era Stratocaster to their catalogue is the Hendrix connection. The world is full of guitarists that still love Jimi Hendrix, so the Custom Shop added a 1969 model as a selling point for all the Hendrix fans. The only colours available for this type of Stratocaster are black, white and sunburst; maple and rosewood is available with finish relic, NOS or closet classic. These are the three colours of Stratocaster Jimi usually is pictured with.

This type of guitar is aged in such a way as to give the buyer the idea that, had Hendrix not left us in 1970, his guitar may well have looked like this one, having done many gigs in its time and showing its age. The other interesting feature is the headstock front; this is considerably darker than the rest of the neck. This is due to the fact that with late-1960s Stratocasters, for an unknown reason, the headstock front was finished in nitrocellulose, similar to that which the early 60s and 50s Stratocasters had all over the necks. The rest of the neck was finished in a polyester mix, hence the darkening of the headstock front and the rest of the neck staying pale in comparison. This type of Stratocaster is aimed at the player who wants a real Hendrix vibe. The four replicas of Hendrix's Woodstock Stratocaster made by the Custom Shop are different to this model as there is not as much aging done, and the clones were clones, in the sense of having every ding and knock done by Jimi, as well as having the pickups made to the exact specifications as the original. This is the archetypal Hendrix Stratocaster made for a player.

This guitar has a period correct black Tolex case with the amp logo added to the side, as well as the mandatory Custom Shop case candy – a fine-looking Stratocaster.

Since the innovation of relic guitars, many luthiers and guitar manufacturers have caught on and have decided to make battered versions of their own guitars, for example, ESP, Gibson and even Martin. The majority age their guitars differently. The relic aspect of guitars appeals to the guitarist who cannot afford a vintage instrument with all the years of abuse, but will still stand for hours in guitar shops staring at a

worn guitar, wondering where the marks came from – whether a Stratocaster was left in the back of a van to be used at sound check testing amps out or thrown around a club in Texas. The mind is a powerful tool for guitarists when considering a £15,000 investment; however, it is not so powerful when faced with a loved one questioning the price!

The Custom Shop is the ultimate Fender dream factory for many Stratocaster or Telecaster fans. The ownership of a genuine vintage Fender has had its game raised by the collectors' market, with worn and cherished vintage guitars fetching high prices. The majority of guitar players cannot afford a vintage model so the Custom Shop relic series fills a gap. The relic series adds a different twist by making guitars that are highly prized by their owners, but are also ideal to take out and gig without the owner worrying about the wear and tear – after all, the guitar is already pretty well worn!

The argument against relics tends to be that of seasoned pros, who once owned a vintage guitar and sold it years back for little money, complaining that the new 'relics' are nonsense and that the majority of pros would have loved nothing more than an expensive, shiny, new Stratocaster in the early days. To them it seems ridiculous that in later years the same company makes expensive battered Stratocasters for what would seem like a lot more money. The guitar world has always been plagued by cash flow problems, with the coolest things being the most expensive; in this respect things have not changed one bit. Stratocaster fans wanting Custom Shop instruments have the initial £1,000+ to consider before even getting a second hand model. Things were no different back in the 1950s or 60s with only the rich owning genuine Fenders.

To many guitar players, other Fender Stratocasters in the current range are all they need. A USA Standard Stratocaster will sound right, play right and look right and for a lot less money than a Custom Shop. The same applies to USA vintage models, which are considered by many to be the top of the standard Fender range, next to the Signature models, which are one step away from the Custom Shop itself. The Custom Shop has always remained the place to go if you want a period-correct guitar or a complete custom job for yourself. The Custom Shop will make anything Fender you want.

The Custom Shop's main guitars have been and will always be the Time Machine series – pick a Strat, pick a year, pick how much wear and tear you want, pay your money and await delivery. The Time Machine series proves what everyone already knew about Fender Stratocasters; they got them right the first time and have not bettered it since. To prove a point, Fender's latest Stratocaster with all the 'NEW AND IMPROVED' features retails at around £800, while the fine example of the Custom Shop's output show here will set you back around £2,000 and is based on a guitar made over fifty years ago.

Whether or not Fender just jumped on the gravy train that is the vintage collectors' market is unsure, but a good Custom Shop Stratocaster can be treasured just as much as a genuine vintage model in the right hands.

# APPENDIX

Should you be lucky to join the likes of Hendrix, Clapton, Vaughan, Marvin and Cray in owning a real Fender Stratocaster, whether a 1950s, 1960s, 1970s or any American-made instrument, your guitar will have a serial number. Serial numbers vary quite significantly.

Those on any Stratocaster are very useful for providing information about your guitar, and are invaluable in the event of theft or forgery. A serial number can provide great insight. The lists should help to date your Fender Stratocaster to its exact year and series.

| 1950s MODELS | SERIAL NUMBERS |
|---|---|
| 1950–54 | Up to 6,000 |
| 1954–56 | Up to 10,000 |
| 1955–56 | 10,000s |
| 1957 | 10,000–20,000s |
| 1958 | 20,000–30,000s |
| 1959 | 30,000–40,000s |

| 1970s MODELS | SERIAL NUMBERS |
|---|---|
| 1971–72 | 300,000s |
| 1973 | 300,000s–500,000s |
| 1974–75 | 400,000s–500,000s |
| 1976 (two variations) | 500,000s–700,000s, |
| | 76 + 5 digits |
| | S6 + 5 digits |
| 1977 (two variations) | S7 + 5 digits |
| | S8 + 5 digits |
| 1978 (three variations) | S7 + 5 digits |
| | S8 + 5 digits |
| | S9 + 5 digits |
| 1979 (two variations) | S9 + 5 digits |
| | E0 + 5 digits |

| 1960s MODELS | SERIAL NUMBERS |
|---|---|
| 1960 | 40,000–50,000 |
| 1961 | 50,000–70,000 |
| 1962 | 60,000–90,000 |
| 1963 | 80,000–90,000 |
| 1963 | (early L-series) 90,000s–L10,000s |
| 1963 | (L-series) L10,000s–L20,000s |
| 1964 | (L-series) L20,000s–L50,000s |
| 1965 | (end of L-series) L50,000s–L90,000s |
| 1965 | 100,000s |
| 1966–67 | 100,000s–200,000s |
| 1968 | 200,000s |
| 1969–70 | 200,000–300,000s |

| 1980s MODELS | SERIAL NUMBERS |
|---|---|
| 1980 (three variations) | S9 + 5 digits / E0 + 5 digits / E1 + 5 digits |
| 1981 (three variations) | S9 + 5 digits / E0 + 5 digits / E1 + 5 digits |
| 1982 (five variations) | E1+ 5 digits / E2 + 5 digits / E3 + 5 digits |
| 1982 (Stratocasters in the vintage series) | V + 4 , 5 or 6 digits (52' tele – pencil neck date) |
| 1983 | E2 + 5 digits / E3 + 5 digits / V + 4, 5, or 6 digits |
| 1984 (three variations) | E3 + 5 digits / E4 + 5 digits / V + 4, 5 or 6 digits |
| 1985 (three variations) | E3 + 5 digits / E4 + 5 digits / V + 4, 5 or 6 digits |
| 1986 | V + 4, 5, or 6 digits |
| 1987 | E4 + 5 digits / V + 4, 5 or 6 digits |
| 1988 | E4 + 5 digits / V + 4 , 5 or 6 digits |
| 1989 | E8 + 5 digits / E9 + 5 digits / V + 4, 5 or 6 digits |

| 1990s AND 2000s MODELS | SERIAL NUMBERS |
|---|---|
| 1990 (four variations) | E9 + 5 digits / N9 + 5 digits / N0 + 5 digits / V + 5 or 6 digits |
| 1991 (three variations) | N0 + 5 digits / N1 + 5 or 6 digits / V + 5 or 6 digits |
| 1992 (three variations) | N1 + 5 or 6 digits / N1 + 5 or 6 digits / V + 5 or 6 digits |
| 1993 (three variations) | N2 + 5 or 6 digits / N3 + 5 or 6 digits / V + 5 or 6 digits |
| 1994 (three variations) | N3 + 5 or 6 digits / N4 + 5 or 6 digits / V + 5 or 6 digits |
| 1995 (three variations) | N4 + 5 or 6 digits / N5 + 5 or 6 digits / V + 5 or 6 digits |
| 1996 (three variations) | N5 + 5 or 6 digits / N6 + 5 or 6 digits / V + 5 or 6 digits |
| 1997 (three variations) | N6 + 5 or 6 digits / N7 + 5 or 6 digits / V + 5 or 6 digits |
| 1998 (three variations) | N7 + 5 or 6 digits / N8 + 5 or 6 digits / V + 5 or 6 / V + 5 or 6 digits |
| 1999 (three variations) | N8 + 5 or 6 digits / N9 + 5 or 6 digits / V + 5 or 6 digits |
| 2000 (four variations) | N9 + 5 or 6 digits / Z0 + 5 or 6 digits / American Deluxe series DZ0 + 5 or 6 digits / V + 5 or 6 digits |
| 2001 (four variations) | Z0 + 5 or 6 digits / Z1 + 5 or 6 digits / American Deluxe Series DZ1 + 5 or 6 digits / V + 5 or 6 digits |
| 2002 (four variations) | Z1 + 5 or 6 digits / Z2 + 5 or 6 digits / American Deluxe Series DZ2 / V + 5 or 6 digits |
| 2003 (four variations) | Z2 + 5 or 6 digits / Z3 + 5 or 6 digits / American Deluxe Series DZ3 + 5 or 6 digits / V + 5 or 6 digits |
| 2004 (four variations) | Z3 + 5 or 6 digits / Z4 + 5 or 6 digits / American Deluxe DZ4 + 5 or 6 digits / V + 5 or 6 digits |
| 2005 (five variations) | Z4 + 5 or 6 digits / Z5 + 5 or 6 digits/ American Deluxe DZ5 + 5 or 6 digits / V + 5 or 6 digits / XN5 + 4 digits (new American vintage) |

| OTHER SPECIFIC MODELS | SERIAL NUMBERS |
|---|---|
| Tribute series Stratocasters (i.e. Hendrix tribute Stratocaster) | Guitars from any type of tribute series begin with TN(xxxxx). These guitars are serial numbered to the specific guitar and can be dated with knowledge that the number only stretches to the model used. |
| California Series guitars, 1997–98 | These guitars all bear the serial number AMXN + 6 digits |
| American Deluxe Stratocasters, 1998–99 | DN + 6 digits |
| Signature series Stratocasters, 1988–2002 | SE8 – 1988<br>SE9 – 1989<br>SN0 – 1990<br>SN1 – 1991<br>SN2 – 1992 (etc)<br>SZ0 – 2000<br>SZ1 – 2001<br>SZ2 – 2002 |
| 35th anniversary Stratocaster | 3 digits of 500 |
| Gold Stratocaster, 1981–83 | G0 + xxxxx |
| Walnut Stratocaster, 1981–83 | CC + xxxxx |

Custom Shop Stratocasters vary widely across the range, so it is worth checking that the guitar has a Custom Shop certificate that has been properly stamped and signed. The certificate should feel as good as the guitar and bear the signature of whoever was the Custom Shop manager at the time.

For more information on serial number information see Fender's extensive website *http://www.fender.com/support/product_dating.php*.

# FURTHER INFORMATION

## Magazines

*UniVibes*
(international magazine devoted to the life and work
of Jimi Hendrix)
Via Delle Corti 11, 51020 Popiglio (PT), Italy
www.univibes.com

*Guitar and Bass*
IPC Country & Leisure Media Ltd, Leon House,
233 High Street, Croydon, CR9 1HZ, UK
www.guitarmagazine.co.uk/index.htm

*Guitar World*
149 5th Avenue, 9th Floor, New York, NY 10010, USA
http://www.guitarworld.com

*Guitar Buyer*
Davenport Publishing Ltd, Alexander House,
38 Forehill, Ely, Cambs, CB7 4ZA, UK
www.guitarbuyermag.com

## Websites

www.musicground.com
The online home of the Music Ground shops in
London, Leeds and Manchester.

www.myspace.com/listentosupernought
The website of the author's own band.

www.stratcollector.com
An invaluable resource for the Stratocaster fan.

www.musicradar.com
Musicians' website.

www.fender.com
The official Fender website.

www.soundsgreatmusic.com
Online shop for guitars and accessories.

# INDEX